WITHDRAWN

SACRED
FIREPLACE

SACRED FIREPLACE
(Oceti Wakan)

Life and Teachings of a
Lakota Medicine Man

Pete S. Catches, Sr.
Edited by Peter V. Catches

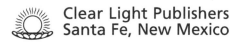 **Clear Light Publishers**
Santa Fe, New Mexico

With much love and devotion, I dedicate this book to Okawinga Win (Perpetual Cycle Woman), Amelia Emily Ribsman Catches, and all wakunka *(elders) who hold the eternal female embodiment of the Great Mystery's infinity of love. It is they who teach* wakanyeja *(sacred beings, children) into adulthood. In the Spotted Eagle Clan and the Sundance Nation, Okawinga Win's spirit lives as a true and loving flower of a matriarch forever in bloom.*

—Peter V. Catches (Zintkala Oyate)

>>>→ • ←‹‹‹

© 1999 by Peter V. Catches
Clear Light Publishers
823 Don Diego, Santa Fe, New Mexico 87501
WEB: www.clearlightbooks.com

First Edition
10 9 8 7 6 5 4 3 2 1

Library of Congress Cataloging-in-Publication Data

Catches, Pete
    Sacred fireplace : life and teachings of a Lakota medicine man / Pete Catches ; edited by Peter V. Catches.
        p.   cm.
    ISBN 1-57416-036-2
    1. Catches, Pete. 2. Oglala Indians—Religion. 3. Oglala Indians—Biography. 4. Shamans—South Dakota Biography.
    I. Catches, Peter (Peter V.) II. Title.
    E99.03C38   1999
    978'.0049752'0092—dc21
    [B]   99-38800
                                                                        CIP

Photographs © Peter V. Catches collection: pages xii, 10, 24, 36, 70, 92, 128, 134, 158, 162, 172, 184, 188, 198, 210, 216, 222
Editor: Barbara Kohl
Book Interior Design/Production: Carol O'Shea
Cover Design: Marcia Keegan and Carol O'Shea
Printed in Canada

CONTENTS

FOREWORD

By Peter V. Catches (Zintkala Oyate)

The words in this book are from Lakotas speaking in an oral tradition. The type of editing undertaken retains the spirit and energy of the language, which embody and derive from the natural philosophy inherent in the culture of the *Lakota oyate*. Previous books about the Lakota people have been devoid of the quality in which these people interact, thereby distorting the full meaning of their language and mindset. Something is lost when English syntax is formed around written translations of the Lakota as well as the words spoken by a person who thinks in Lakota. What we have attempted here is to keep the interpretation as authentic as possible.

PREFACE

By Peter V. Catches (Zintkala Oyate)

When I was a young boy, we lived at a place called
Calico, a village between three and four miles northwest of the town of Pine Ridge, South Dakota, on
Highway 18. The Calico Meeting Hall is now a large,
dilapidated, one-room log house, with two chimneys on
each side and three sixty-foot tall cottonwood trees in
front. The White Clay Creek flows on the same side of
the highway as the meeting hall. Evidence of change
lies to the north, where in the foothills covered with
beautiful pine trees is a church near a white cliff known
as White Bank.

　　The story goes that one Easter a boy relative gave
me a gift of a raccoon. I guess they didn't let the boy keep
it because the raccoon got into everything. As soon as
this relative told me the raccoon was mine, I fell completely in love with it. Some of you are familiar with the
mannerisms of these beautiful, furry little creatures.
They are a wonder to watch, particularly for little children. When you give raccoons something, they tend to
wash it with their humanlike hands, or so it seems—it's a
habit that makes an amusing sight. So, there I was in the
middle of the floor in our house gleefully playing with
my new pet, oblivious to my surroundings.

》》》→ • ←《《《

Late in the day, my mother told me to put my still unnamed pet outside. Although I begged for the raccoon to stay inside, my pleas fell on deaf ears. The raccoon had to sleep outside. The door to our house faced south, and eight yards from the door was a shade. A type of shelter, the shade was a square, ribbed structure with pine boughs on the top and sides, and was used only in the summer. That night I tied my lovable little pet to the shade. I put out a little blanket and a bowl of water with some bread and gave the raccoon a few last pets with a loving goodnight.

The next morning my happiness was obliterated. My pet raccoon had committed suicide! The other kids mocked. Nothing of this magnitude had ever happened in my young life. I was devastated and I didn't know what to do. Somehow, I found the courage to loosen the tiny rope that held my pet suspended in mid air. I took that little blanket and wrapped his frail little body. My grandfather, who was alive at that time, told me that I must bury my pet, but in the back of my mind, I had a better idea. I said I would wait for my father. When my father came home late that afternoon, I marched right up to him with my wrapped-up raccoon and laid it at his feet. With tears in my eyes, barely able to speak, I demanded that he bring my pet raccoon back to life.

My father's gentle voice explained the matters of life and the inevitable end of everything that lived. Right then and there as a child, I accepted death as a part of our journey back to our real home, the place of the Great

>>>→ • ←<<<

ix

Spirit. Often, with the death of those closest to me, with the sadness and the tears that burn cold on my cheeks, I know that death is a corridor to eternal life.

I would like to take this opportunity to thank all the people who have so generously contributed to bringing this book to publication. May the Great Mystery bless each of you for your efforts. I want to especially acknowledge and thank my friend and nephew, Robert I. Holden, for the many hours he spent taping and transcribing the words of my father, Petaga Yuha Mani.

—Peter V. Catches (Zintkala Oyate)

Peter V. Catches giving blessing.

Pete Catches and grandson Robert Holden, 1990.

INTRODUCTION

By Peter V. Catches (Zintkala Oyate)

Petaga Yuha Mani, known as Pete S. Catches, Sr., was considered a holy man of the Dakota Nation. As a thirty-seventh generation medicine man of the Spotted Eagle Clan, he taught the fundamental aspects of teachings, understandings, and ceremonies of Canku Lute, the Red Road of Life, or the Pipe religion, as it is known by the Lakota people. This book can help guide the reader who has an open heart.

Pete Catches, Sr., was most well known for bringing the Wiwangyang Wacipi (Sundance) into the open in the early 1960s. The Sundance and certain other Lakota rituals were driven underground in the late 1800s. For many years, people found practicing these rituals were subject to a $10,000 fine and/or a ten-year prison sentence.

Pete Catches' commitment to returning the Sundance to the lives of the Lakota was a courageous act that gained much love and appreciation from the minds, hearts, and spirits of the Lakota people. During this time he refused many offers by people who wished to collaborate with him to write a book about his life and work, because he felt that the time was not right. Now, in the pages of *Sacred Fireplace*, you will find glimpses of the devastation of an ancient culture, the deep-rooted sorrow of reservation life, and the rebirth of the Lakota oyate. Pete Catches had a dream, or spiritual vision, of a healing center for all people, called Oceti Wakan (Sacred Fireplace).

The Spotted Eagle Way

Petaga Yuha Mani's way of medicine is called the Spotted Eagle Way. I too follow that way of doctoring. Although similar in nature, my ability in the way was by birthright and developed differently from that of my father. At my father's request, I wrote the following characterization of the Eagle Way.

Lakota people belong to different clans, such as the Bear Clan, the Elk Clan, and the Heyoka Clan (people who literally do things backward in a humorous manner and whose spirit helpers are the powerful Thunder Beings). There are also ghost healers (medicine men specialized in exorcism), who do not belong to a particular clan. Each clan has its own medicine way used to help clan constituents. And each way has respective ceremonies and doctorings that are part of the clan's way of life in this world and of their conception of the spirit world.

My father and I are of the Spotted Eagle Clan. In the Eagle Way, everything is done in the light so that everyone can see, such as the Seven Sacred Rites given to us by

Wohpe, daughter of Taku Skan Skan, which include the Purification Rite, Pipefast, Sundance, and healing ceremonies to find missing loved ones and to help people who are emotionally, mentally, spiritually, and physically ill. We do not hide behind covered windows or darkness.[1] Because our truths and beliefs are simple, we gain a faith that can move mountains. The Eagle's Way is the most powerful in the realms of heaven; it soars high above all others in Lakota society.

THE BLESSING

In an age long ago, there was a teacher of realms beyond.
It was his nature to follow the Eagle's Way
in ultimate reality of truth, and to behold
Wakan Tanka's enlightenment of the absolute.

The warrior walked and came upon a gathering. He was searching for inner peace, relief from the brutality of his life. He was searching for answers to the questions that intruded upon his mind from the sadness of his cold heart. He knew of death and how his footsteps were replaced by its shadow. He knew that his loneliness kept him isolated as well as safe.

The gathering was a great coming together of spiritual teachers from many different peoples, cultures, and beliefs. Each teacher had a retinue of singers, drummers, and helpers, and each retinue wore such beautiful regalia that it was hard to distinguish which was the most magnificent. The sacred songs were done in harmonious splendor, touching the hearts of the many and causing joyous tears to flow, but the warrior remained untouched. He saw that some people were totally elated to be at this gathering, but nothing at all stirred in him.

The warrior looked beyond the magnificent display and the sonorous words and saw that none of the teachers radiated the spiritual beauty that comes from the Great Mystery. He saw that none were inspired by the eternal virtue that comes from the deity of the brave.[2] An earthly desire to be universally liked was their real ambition, and their only contribution was to please themselves. Untouched by their words, he grew angry at their falseness.

Disillusioned and disheartened, he turned away. His melancholy thoughts floundered in a sea of hopelessness where there is no love of existence. He felt powerless in a world not his own. Dimly he heard the announcer of the gathering asking for everyone's attention. "We have the final speaker," the announcer said, "a man who is the keeper of the Spotted Eagle Way." The warrior turned back to look at this last speaker and saw no entourage, no beautiful regalia. Instead, the man wore a simple ribbon shirt and a few eagle feathers in his hair. The warrior saw a man whose body and soul bore the scars of living, yet vibrated with an outpouring of energy. Feeling a strange but powerful attraction, the warrior moved closer to the center of the gathering, eager to hear the man's words. He could tell that this speaker would bless the gathering with a glimpse of the truth.

"People of the Creator," this final speaker began, "I ask you now for a moment of serene silence. In this silence pray for your love, for your life, and how you want that love to become real, for how you want to embrace life and live free, building your love slowly and feeling it grow." The warrior opened his heart to let those few words ignite a gentle understanding and felt the silence beginning.

"Fulfill the obligations that are right for you alone," the speaker continued. "They may not be many; yet be certain that you complete them in the path of your footsteps."

The warrior's mind traveled back to a long-forgotten time. He recalled clearly his childhood dream, a dream that nourished and promised a cherished tomorrow. He was filled with anguish for having betrayed his soul.

"That small inspiration begins to grow in the earth of your being," the speaker said. "It is an enlightened joy that comes from God. Knowing this, moment by moment, it becomes holy. In order to build that love, you do it day by day until, when you stand before the Great Mystery, you can say, 'My God, my love, I have built my love slowly. For my love to become real, I have worked honestly so that which I have built and attained is forever, and in your love.'"

A tear trickled from the warrior's eye and rolled warmly down his face. The silence had truly begun. It was a blessed moment.

"Today," the speaker went on, "I stand before you, people of the Great Mystery, an advocate of the Sundance Nation, whose members are the people of peace. We all know there is a sunburst of light coming from the Creator.

Each ray of light is a truth, a way of wisdom and livelihood through which each culture worships our Creator. We know God is God, and the Creator's essence is the holy swirl of this universe. Therefore, we must acknowledge and accept that we as individuals are integral to the fabric of His holy design."

The warrior felt he was at a threshold. The feelings of foreboding and anxiety that clouded his daily life were suddenly lifted and a sweet innocence took its place. He felt an awkward outpouring of change that warmed his cold heart.

"As you were told," the speaker said, "I am of the Spotted Eagle Way, one of the clans of the Lakota people. I come here not by coincidence, but rather through a clear imprint of my footsteps in the path of my destiny. For some of you, the meaning of what I am obliged to say here will be more than you will be able to comprehend in this moment, yet the solution will remain with you until you are ready for it to flower within you. For others, it will be a profound sweetness of knowledge that you have been waiting for all of your lives, and are now eager to embrace and accept. To find and draw that hidden curtain in your mind, look behind your insipid color to find the complete sacredness of the one holy fire of love, and leave that door open in your heart."

The warrior did not understand these words until he glanced around the gathering. Although he saw the differences in height and size among the assembled people, he most clearly saw differences in shades of color. He closed his eyes and saw the darkness, and then something wonderful happened. He heard the sounds of the people, divided by their different beliefs and cultures, yet sharing an equality fed by the fire of life the Great Mystery so lovingly fashioned in their souls.

"The place where we are living now," the simple man continued, "this in-between world of worlds, this tangible reality of our known lives and the limits of our comprehension, this is what we know to be true scientifically, as our senses grasp this truth as fact. But as we stand at the altar of our quest for understanding, here below the clouds of fearful holiness, we are in the presence of the sacred gentle and loving mother of our sentient beings."

The warrior's eyes opened to a new level of consciousness, to a world that he never imagined. The cold, dark, and unloved vortex of his once lonely existence vanished. Its laws and beliefs and the false greed of his ambitions lay burned to ashes by his metamorphosis, by his realization that his soul was a part of the sacred fire of the Great Mystery.

"In this whole world," the simple man said, "there is no place sacred. There is only one place sacred for you and from that place you will speak to the Great Mystery. In that place, the Great Spirit will listen to your words. It is from there that the Great Mystery has made your words holy. It is there that eternal love grows, there that the Most Holy turns to look at you…. My time is up. I pray that the Great Spirit's love and affection are forever yours. *Mitakuye oyasin.*"

>>>→ • ←<<<

The warrior watched as this simple man, who had healed and changed his life forever, walked away through the crowd. His past was already an eternity away and forgotten. The warrior faced a bright tomorrow on an ancient but new road, the Red Road of Life.

A spiritual man of the Eagle's Way embodies the way: he has integrity, character, honor, reason, natural conduct,[3] intelligence, and wisdom. He is able to assist others in achieving unity with the Great Mystery, regardless of their situations.[4] This spiritual man is reserved. He conforms to Wakan Tanka and thus achieves favor with power. With power, everything is possible. A spiritual man of the Eagle's Way knows the limit and extent of his abilities in accordance with spiritual laws, as well as when to impose these laws on others.

People often do not understand this Red Road of Life because they crave intellectual knowledge. Being Lakota, following the Red Road of Life, is to live in balance and harmony. To know this ancient concept is a step toward the Eagle's Way, which is as deep and vast as the immortal. Out of Wakan Tanka comes the Eagle's Way, and from the Eagle's Way comes unity. Out of unity come peace, healing, and harmony. When the way of the Eagle is lost, unity gives way to compassion. When compassion fades, justice without feeling or emotion prevails. And then, when justice without feeling fades, ceremonial rituals abound with the loss of self.[5]

In the Eagle's Way foreknowledge of what will come is both good and bad. The wise person takes the good and leaves the bad, and humbly lives in the Eagle's Way. Evil is thus irrelevant—it retains power, but is unable to harm the people.

My father, Petaga Yuha Mani, asked me to share the Spotted Eagle Way in this simple fashion. I thank you for reading this from me, and may the Great Spirit's love and affection brighten your life and the lives of your loved ones.

Petaga Yuha Mani praying during marriage ceremony.

One *(Wanji)*
LIFE TEACHINGS
& EXPERIENCES

This is the winter of 1989, and I am seventy-seven years old. I am Pete Catches, Sr., known in the Indian world as Petaga Yuha Mani (He Walks with Hot Coals). I am an Oglala Lakota, born and raised on the Pine Ridge Indian Reservation. I still live on the reservation, and hope to be here until the end of my life.

From these windows of seventy-seven years of life, I have watched the world pass before me. Many times, especially very early in the morning when I wake up, I lie awake and look back over the years to when I was a kid.

I was born to Paul and Anna Catches The Enemy at Manderson, South Dakota, which is located between Pine Ridge and Porcupine. My grandmother's name was Her Red Horses, and my grandfather's name was Big Ribs. At that time in the life of my grandfather and grandmother, most of the people did not have first names, but went by their childhood names instead. Many brothers and sisters had different surnames.

As a kid, I lived in Grass Creek, way back in the country between Manderson and Oglala. We had to go several miles to a spring that was cold in the summer. We would make a special trip to the spring on horseback to bring back cold water to enjoy in the heat. Nowadays, we don't have to travel so far for cold water. We have many things that make life easier for us that were absent from our early lives.

I lost both my father and mother when I was very young. I do not recall my *unci* (grandmother) or *kakala* (grandfather). But I did have an uncle who raised me, who advised me on how to live. When I was seven years old, he taught me when I got up in the morning to put on my clothing and then fix my bed—not to just get up, walk away, and let the blankets lie around. He taught me to take care of those things, because they kept me warm all night. That is showing respect and love for the things you have, even a blanket. He told me that you take care of your cap, because you wear it through the day. He told me to show respect for my clothing by hanging it up, not to throw it here and there. Another thing he told me was that when I borrow something, I must show respect and be sure to return it.

My uncle taught me about pride in the Lakota people and about traditional ways. Long after the kerosene lamp was blown out at night, he would ask me, "*Tunska* (nephew), are you awake?" And I would say, "Yes." Then he would begin talking about the things that came to his mind, the things that were good for me to do. He said, "When you walk along to the neighbors on an errand, as you walk along the creek and there is a stick of wood, perhaps six or seven feet long, you break off the other branches and carry that. When you come upon another one, you break off the branches and carry the length of it. You carry two or three, and when you arrive at the neighbor's on whatever errand you are on, take it to the woodpile. If you see an axe there, chop these branches to the length of a cooking stove, carry them inside, and place them beside the stove. When you take a dipperful of water to drink, if you see the water is getting low—usually there are two buckets there, maybe sometimes three—you take the one that has less water in it, pour it into another bucket, go outside to the barrel or the pump and bring in a bucketful for the household. In doing these small things, even though you are not told to do so, these people will be kind to you. They will see that you did not just go there to loaf or sit around."

My uncle said, "When I wake you in the morning, you get up. Do not have me holler at you a second time. When you hear my voice, just get up. After you do that two or three times, it will become a habit. It will be easier for you to get up in the morning. But thinking that you will take another minute or so in sleep or lying down, taking it easy, and getting up slowly, indicates your laziness. So, when you hear my voice, just get up."

He taught me a lot of things. I went with him one morning to look for the horses. The lead horse—called the mother horse in our language, sometimes the oldest mare in a group of horses—has a bell around its neck, and they call them bell horses. He said, "This is what you do. That rope hanging by the side of the door, take that down and follow the trail to the hill. Just follow behind me."

As we walked along and came to the crest of the hill, he said, "What you do next is listen good for a time, a space of time, and wait until it is calm, and then holler out loud, as loud as you can. The bell horse, over there in the canyon or wherever, will hear you and move, and you can hear the bell. Follow that sound and you will find the horses. So, early in the morning when you get up on the hill, you stand there listening. You may barely hear that bell because in the morning, whether they are lying down or standing up, they are asleep. But if you can hear that bell, you can follow the sound and find where the horses are."

In that group of horses was one whose coat was an odd color. We called him by his nickname, Sihanskala, which means "long feet," because his back hooves were kind of slender. When he walked, you could see the tracks—it seemed as if somebody in moccasins went through there. I would go up to him, talking all the while, and he would just stand there. He loved to be talked to and petted. I would pet him all over, even down to his feet. He would look down to his ankle and he would be looking at me, his head over the other way, but still looking at me. I would also pull on his tail; he liked that too. He would turn his head one way or the other, showing his pleasure. Finally, I would put my rope around his neck, lead him to the side of a hill or to a little bank somewhere, find a place there, and jump on top of him. Then we would bring the other horses to the watering place in the canyon, water them, and take them to the corral. By that time, the sun would have risen.

All of this work would happen in the morning before sunrise, and I got used to that. I loved to be outside before sunup to inhale the freshness of the air, to be able to wake up the birds. Many times I was out there on the trail before they started singing.

My uncle taught me about paying attention. He said, "Be obedient. When you go someplace, to a neighbor's, see what the woman of the house is doing. If she is cooking, go to the woodpile, and if there is no cut wood, try to cut some. If you cannot cut wood, get some wood chips, a bucket of chips, and replenish her fire. See what else you can do." In this way, my uncle told me, "people will love you—they will know that you are eager to help."

So, that is how I started my life. Later, when I went out to work on a ranch or on a farm, I would ask to do more than what I was allotted. If I were driving a tractor, plowing a field, or feeding cattle in the wintertime, I would ask to milk the family cow or feed the chickens or the hogs. I spent long hours going out of my way to do the chores of the family farm or the ranch, besides the work I would normally do each day.

I worked seven days a week on some jobs. I worked on one particular ranch for several summers. I volunteered to make the rounds of the windmills on Sunday mornings, take salt out there in a pickup. If I remember right, there were seventeen windmills on that ranch. Even though some repairs were needed around the windmills, I could not get to all of them in one day. So I would continue my work the following Sunday. Some Sundays I would mount a horse and ride the outside fence, checking it. If I saw a break in the fence, when I returned the next week my first task would be to go and repair it.

My uncle also taught me to be honest and to be kind. He taught me how to be generous. He said, "Generosity is not just giving; generosity is sharing. Generosity to me is visiting the sick when you have other things to do, but you put that aside and go visit the sick. That to me is the greatest generosity, to put aside some things you should do and go visit the sick." I have done this many times throughout my life.

Instead of having an unci, a grandmother, I had my uncle to teach me many good things in life.[6] He told me, "Never try to imitate somebody; just try to be you. Live in this world the way Wakan Tanka (the Great Spirit), Tunkasila (Grandfather), fashioned for you to live, because you can never be what you are not. Even though you try hard to be what you are not, you will never be what you were not made for."

As I grew up, I began to understand these words. "Do not try to be what you are not." Those very small words are very strong. One of the things he taught me was that I would never be a white man, a *wasicu*, so I should not be imitating the white man's way. Even though I eat his food and use his way of clothing, forever and ever I will be a Lakota, because I talk Lakota, and I live the Lakota way. I am a medicine man, and the white man cannot ever be what I am. He may learn how to talk Lakota. He may try to imitate me by living the Lakota way, but never in this life, in this world, will he be a Lakota like I am.

These are the things my uncle taught me. I did not fully grasp the meaning, the full intent, of what he taught me until later on in life. When I was a young man, during the time he was still teaching me, he too passed away. Looking back, I wish that I could have lived side by side with him for many years before his final end. His name was William Cedar Face. He was very well known. He was very expressive when he talked Lakota. So I had an Indian, a Lakota, training and teaching me, and I think I still keep parts of these things in my life today. My belief is like that.

Traditionally, the family circle—what we know as *tiyospaye* (community)—provides security for people in Indian culture. In Indian families, children are naturally bashful. To other people who may come as visitors, it might seem as if the children were backward. But within the family circle, we understood what unity was. We loved one another, we would come to each other, we helped each other, and we shared everything that we had. I have known instances where a family member was not present at the time we were fortunate to receive a small bucket of plums or cherries. We would see to it that a portion of the fruit was saved for the absent member of the family. Being a family for us means that all partake of what there is to eat.

When I refer to tradition, I am speaking of the Red Road of Life, the language that we speak, and the belief of the Sacred Pipe. We use this belief system to guide our lives.

In comparison, in today's lifestyle that we know under this dominant society, everything is turned way around. Children now might not share with each other. I realize that children are thoughtless. If a family member is not with them at the time that they have ice cream or pie, many do not save a portion for the absent member.

How the world has changed under this dominant society! The sense of value, honesty, and truthfulness is gone from our people. Others may say that it is still here, but no. I see these changes happening not only on the Pine Ridge Reservation but also wherever I go on other reservations.

So much of our way of life is being lost. Honor and respect are two of the things that we Lakota hold in high esteem. For example, when we go to a wake, it is to pay our last respects. When I was a boy, I did not know what death was. Children were forbidden to go to a wake, and especially to a funeral. The old ones wanted us to live a long time, and during childhood, they did not want us to see them crying at a funeral. This is one tradition that is absolutely gone from our people today. You go to pay your respects nowadays and all you see are children running around without supervision. Their mothers and dads sit there not noticing. Children go out the door and the next minute they go back inside as though it was a recreation area; they are practically stepping on your toes. At the cemetery you will see children standing right there at the gravesite, looking down at the coffin being lowered into that hole.

Why do we not show respect by keeping our children at home? People may see this in other, nontraditional ways.

They might say, "We want them to get used to these things." But this I did not know when I was a child. This is not the Lakota way of showing respect for the old ones.

I look back on the world that we had. All the streams that flowed through the country were clean and pure, there were virgin forests, and the snow-capped mountains were clean and pure. But after the cry of "westward ho," when the white man came and cities sprung up, everything that we hold dear—the Lakota world—began to crumble. The white men took, and took, and took. Even now, they are after the Black Hills, the only remaining sacred Black Hills that we have, which are protected by the Treaty of 1868.[7]

It is very sad for me to contemplate the issue of the Black Hills. A treaty is supposed to be the highest law of the land. We have had many treaties with the United States government and the government broke every one of those treaties. If they break the Black Hills 1868 Treaty, I think the United States government has no face, no honor, no dignity. We are the aboriginal people of this vast Turtle Island. We are the original people, the landlords. The loss of our land undermines all that we hold dear. The sacred Black Hills are not for sale.

On Religion

I heard one old-timer say that we are gradually being divided through so-called Christianity and education. My early education was at Holy Rosary Mission, now known as Red Cloud Indian School. It is a Jesuit- and Franciscanrun boarding school located on the Pine Ridge Indian Reservation. I attended that school for a number of years. There were many misunderstandings and misconceptions when I was in school, and there was a great culture clash. We came from Indian families, and when we went to school we did not know much about the English language. The only words we were familiar with were "yes" and "no." Sometimes we liked to say "no" or we hollered out "yes" at the wrong times and in the wrong situations, and we would be punished.

The schoolteachers we had in early childhood were not kind. I would not say that they were racist, but rather that they were just plain mean to the Indian boys. I do not know about treatment of the girls because we were completely separated. The boys' section was on one side of the school, the girls' section on the other, and there was a high fence in between. We could not communicate with any of our female relations on the other side, and they, in turn, could not speak to us. There was no visiting of any sort. We were kept strictly apart. That is one of the reasons why I say they were mean.

The Indian boys who were sent to this boarding school were punished when they talked Lakota, our native language. We had long hair by the time school began in the fall, shoulder length or even longer. Many of the boys' hair had not been cut since spring when school was out, and for that we got punished too. As part of the punishment we were cut bald-headed; it was very embarrassing for a boy to be bald-headed at that time.

I would say that religion, prayers, and the English language were forced upon me. They offer these things in a kindly way. A young man taught us every day about a religion, about heaven, hell, and all that it pertains to, in order for us to become believers. Later on, I realized that I was brainwashed. As I grew older, I found that teaching religion forcibly is not a true Christian way of life. But in this Catholic institution, the beliefs about heaven and hell and purgatory and so on were forced into me, and I believed. Even today, I cannot get it out of my mind completely.

I do not understand the reason for the cruel things that they did. They supposedly lived by the Bible and the word of Jesus Christ, that Jesus Christ is the truth, the light of the world, and the way to live. A true Christian would be like Jesus Christ; he would be forgiving, and he would be understanding with sinners, so to speak. But these teachers were not that way. I think they were mean to us because we were Indians.

As a young boy in school, I saw pictures of the Pilgrims back in the 1600s. These Pilgrims were walking two by two; each man with his wife, going to church dressed in their best finery. The men had a Bible under one arm, and on the shoulder on the other side was a gun. That picture remains with me in my mind: this is America. They use that Bible sometimes to divide people.

When I came away from school, I tried to put the way they taught me in perspective in the world that I experienced in my adult life, working among white people in various states, including Colorado, Wyoming, and Nebraska.

SACRED FIREPLACE

Another side of the picture in America is that we are human beings, that each person is an individual, that we can say the things that we want to say, that we can talk Indian if we want to. Why does this Christian institution try to curb all of that? They wanted to do away with our way of life, our culture, our traditions, our language. They wanted to stamp all of that out and make us into something that we know very little of.

One of the treaties signed by the Lakota Nation said that only three denominations were allowed in the Lakota Nation: Presbyterian, Episcopalian, and Roman Catholic. Today we have close to 100 churches in Indian country. I see religion as the system used by the United States government and the church, no matter what denomination, to divide the people. Brothers are divided with this church thing. There are so many churches that Indian people believe in many ways.

I see some people go to church every Sunday, and those same people hate other people. Some of those people who go to churches do not like me when they see me in the street, because I pray with the Pipe. They look at me as an enemy. This Lord Jesus Christ that they believe in, I believe in Him, too. But I believe in Him in a different way. I believe in Jesus Christ as the greatest of medicine men. He said in the Bible to love your neighbors and love your enemies.

I am not saying that these churches are no good. I like a person when he prays, no matter how he prays; and it is the same Creator that all the rest of us pray to. So in a sense, all of these people are good, but only if they do what the Bible preaches, what the Bible says. I see the answers in the Bible. I have read the Bible. John the Baptist preached the coming of Christ in the desert, wearing a camel's hide. In that desert heat he lived on locusts and honey. How many of us could do that for our God? There are other great men of the Bible, like Moses on Sinai. He went up there to pray for forty days and forty nights. The Indian people look on Moses and they say openly that he went on a fast like we do with our Pipe. We go on a fast, but not as long as forty days. The longest we go is four days and four nights, because for us the number four is sacred. The numbers seven, fourteen, and twenty-eight are sacred to us too.

It is very hard to live a traditional life. We eat the white man's food, wear his clothes, speak his language. When I talk English, I hate myself. I would rather talk Lakota because that is how Wakan Tanka made me. He made me for what I am. He gave me a language, a tongue to pray to Him, to talk to Him. He gave me ways to worship Him; that is love, and I know He loves me.

How is it that ages and ages ago—and no one had to tell us this—the Indian people knew there is a Wakan Tanka, a Great Spirit, whom other people call God? Our Wakan Tanka is right here as I talk. He is right here listening to what I am saying, so He knows that what I am saying is the truth. In the message that is going out to the world from this moment, I ask Wakan Tanka to bless those people that receive it, and learn something from it, that maybe even one word from it will cure people of the problems they have.

Pete and friend at Pete's home on the Pine Ridge Reservation, South Dakota.

The Great Spirit's Guiding Hand

Now I will turn to some happenings at various times in my life. Earlier in my life, I was sometimes active in local rodeos, like the ones at Oglala on the Fourth of July, Manderson on the Fourth of July, the Kyle District Fair, the Custer Gold Discovery Days, and the Pine Ridge Oglala Sundance. They had races and rodeos, and I took part in bareback riding in most of the Pine Ridge rodeos. I could have continued in the rodeo circuit if I were not so poor. It takes money for entrance fees, travel, meals, expenses, and I did not have that.

At the time I am talking about, in the late 1930s through the early 1950s, money was hard to come by. You could not find a job during the Depression. A person who wanted to go to a rodeo had to sell his horse or some part of his property, like a saddle, in order to get there. I did not have that kind of stuff. So, I participated to a small extent, but I loved it.

I got injured once at the Kyle District Fair. The horse I was riding seemed to understand when the whistle blew that the ride was over. When the whistle blew, he quit bucking and took off at a run. He was a fast runner. I started to get off; I slung my right leg over the side of the horse. At that moment I heard someone coming, a rider on a gray horse. He said, "Stay on and I will pick you up." I believed him. So, I remained sitting sideways on that fast-running horse. I was constantly sliding back toward the tail, toward the rump of that running horse. I realized the guy that was to pick me up was losing ground. When the chance was good, I braced myself and jumped off. I landed on my right leg, and I somersaulted several times. When I got up, there was a sprain in my knee; the lower portion of my leg from the knee on down was in front of me, and it was going every which way. It would not stand still, so I grabbed hold of it.

That injury lasted quite a while. The local doctor, a Dr. McNeil, who was living in Kyle at that time, doctored me. People knew and liked him. He was sort of an old man, but very successful in what he did. He set my leg in place. Once you wrench the knee joint like that, only the person who experiences it knows the agony and pain that go with it. The doctor gave me a handful of pills, but they did not help. I had to resort to cheap whiskey, called moonshine, to help me deaden that pain. I did not sleep that night or the following night because of the pain. That is the only time I ever got hurt real bad in the rodeos.

Until a few years ago, I broke horses, or trained them, both in harness and saddle. In fact, we had a bunch of horses at the time I was riding rodeo. We had over thirty head that we took care of at the home place. I would bring two or three back for people who wanted me to break their horses. I like to talk to the horses. I like being kind to them, feeding them, petting them, and giving them sugar.

When I brought a wild horse to the home place, people used to say that it would head back for home. But the horses did not return home when I turned them loose. I would tell them, "Stay around here. This is like your home." I would say this to the horse in Lakota. The horses got to know me pretty well, and they would stay.

I loved to work among horses. The last time one bucked with me on its back was when I was sixty years old. It is customary in a family circle that one has to ride out to gather horses early each morning. One Easter Sunday morning, during the time that I worked for the church, we had to go to church later because of what happened with this horse.

Early in the morning, I went to a ridge where I was riding a half-broke horse; his name was Spaniciya (Burnt Himself). I was loping along this ridge, looking this way and that way, searching for the horses. When I came to a point where I was to turn around I slowed down, and just about that time my stirrup broke. And of course, when this half-broke horse saw the whole stirrup flying out to one side, he started bucking in a circle, right on the tip of the ridge.

On both sides of us was a sloping hill. When the horse went out, up, and cat-fished, I thought he was going to sail over the side, but he kept his footing. Sometimes the dirt on the edge of the ridge would give way under the weight of his bucking. Then he would sit down, practically falling over. Then he would get to his feet and start bucking again.

I did not fall off, but that was some ride. When the horse quit bucking, I calmed him down and talked to him. I saw my stirrup lying halfway down the hill. I had to lead my horse over to the broken stirrup. When I finished repairing the stirrup, I went down into the valley to continue searching for horses.

This is part of the way of life that most Indians lived in those days. We did not have to ride in a rodeo. We did not have to have a crowd cheering. That morning when this half-broke horse was jumping under me and turning this way and that way, bucking in a circle, nearly falling down, the only observers were birds. Maybe the Great Spirit reached out His protective hand. This incident was not the only one; I have experienced many more. I know the Great Spirit was there watching over me, even in my foolishness, to see that later on in my life I could be of some use to the people whom I live with in this world.

In many instances in my life, like the one I just related, we had to get to the church at a given time and time was running out. I had to get the horses, search for them, and run them back to the corral. We traveled by wagon and team in those days. But we got to church on time, no matter what, under any circumstances, rain or shine.

Sometimes you run for time, sometimes you get late, or you get bogged down because of something that broke. But all in all, it is the work that really counts, the efforts that you make. It is our belief that as a person you look at the future with faith in yourself. Knowing that you have set a goal to that point in your life, the road that you take, you realize that it is much harder than you thought, but having the will to continue is what counts.

Now I will talk about certain happenings in my life. I sometimes like to remember these episodes, because it was a time when people knew me for what I could do. I was never a bragger; I only talk the truth. These happenings were not sacred things, although you could look at them that way. I know the Great Spirit in His mysterious ways takes care of His people. And by that, I mean that He took care of me. He had a plan for me, a pattern of life. What I am doing is what He intended me to be in my life, a medicine man of the people, of the Oglala Lakota people.

When I was seventeen years old I was working on a farm picking corn. I was privileged to use a team of mules that belonged to this farmer. The whole outfit was the farmer's property: the wagon, the harness, and the team of mules. There was a couple of other Indian camps there, and they, too, were picking corn. One evening I had chores to do at home at the camp. Because we lived in tents and this was in the month of January, it was cold. I had to chop wood for the evening, night, and early morning, and perhaps the next day. So, it was part of my work to come in from the fields early in the evening so that I could chop wood.

On this particular evening, I came in with the team of mules and unloaded my load. I could not pick much corn, since this was the first year that I did any kind of farm work. I had picked potatoes that fall, and then we started picking corn in December. "Shucking corn" is what they say. You take the outer covering of the corn and you break it off and throw the naked corn into the wagon box. Some people are good at it. They would get a load or nearly a load before noon, and by the evening they would get another. But, being my first year picking corn, I only picked around fifteen bushels in half a day. The farmer was paying ten cents a bushel. It was a decent wage that accumulated over a week.

So, I came in early that one particular day. I unloaded my load of corn, took the team of mules to the water tank to drink, and then took the mules to the barn. The first stall belonged to the team of mules. I put the mules in their stall, and I took the harnesses off and hung them on the wall. When I was through, I heard a wagon come in. I went outside and saw workers from one of the other Indian camps who had come in early because they had a load. I went to the driver and said, "You go ahead and unload your load and I will take care of your team." So he said, "Alright," and he started unloading his corn. I unhitched his team and took them to the watering place.

After the team was finished drinking water, I led them into the doorway to the barn near the mules. I walked in, and because the mules were feeding on oats, I guess they did not want to be bothered. The mules heard horses coming in with harnesses jingling and making noise, and they knew it was horses. In their animal way, they did not want horses to come near them, maybe feed on what they were eating. So, I heard something whistling like a strong wind, whoosh, just like that. I turned my head just in time to see one of the mules kicking with both hind hooves. The hooves missed my face by maybe two or three inches, one on each side of my face.

>>>→ • ←<<<

I could not sleep that night, thinking that if I had been just a bit to one side my head would have been smashed against the wall. The mule had backed up; it gave a forceful kick, raising his entire hind end, and kicked out with both legs. His hooves were in line with my face, and the hooves hit the wall. I did not want to go to bed. I even thought that if I went to sleep, I would die. Maybe it was what they refer to as shock.

And by this I knew, thinking back on the incident years later, that this Wakan Tanka fashions our lives for us. And whether we are being foolish or not, He saves us from leaving this world. He wants us to do something in life—something good, something pleasing, something that is very enriching to be in harmony with our fellow man.

Another occasion was the Saturday before Easter of that year. I had a friend, Silas Left Hand Bull, working at the Holy Rosary Mission as a secretary and bookkeeper at the time. I went to the mission, and while I was there, he said, "I'm glad you have come, because I want to hire you to go to Chadron (Nebraska). I phoned over there to the greenhouse, and they are going to prepare two sets of lilies for the mass on Easter Sunday at the church."

I agreed to go. At that time, you could buy gas at the mission gas pump. He gave me money, I drove over there to the gas pump, and they filled the tank for me. The attendant checked the oil and gave me extra oil. I told Silas, "I will go home and get prepared and I will come early. We will start as soon as you are finished with your office work."

I went home and told my wife that we had to go to Chadron, that Silas had bought some lilies for the altar for Easter Sunday Mass. My wife said, "Can I go along? I want to buy some things at the store." I said, "All right. That will be good. We will make it one trip." So, we came early to the mission. When Silas got off work, we took a cut-across to White Clay and another through Beaver Creek. At the side of Beaver Wall there is a road that cuts through to Hay Springs and one that branches to Chadron. We went through there.

It was late when we got to Chadron. We drove directly to the greenhouse. The light was on and we went in. Someone had the order all prepared, a whole bunch of lilies, two sets, for Easter Sunday Mass. The lilies were put in a pasteboard box so they would not get crushed, and we put them in the back trunk. We went to a restaurant on the main street of Chadron for supper, and then my wife did some shopping.

We started out late and we did not want to have trouble on the road. The cut-across was a gravel road, but most of it was muddy. So, we took the paved route going through Hay Springs, Rushville, and then north to White Clay, Pine Ridge, and Holy Rosary Mission. There are lots of trees there, and the road kind of winds around, but it is a good highway.

On the way back, right at Border Creek, up ahead was a loaded semi. It was traveling slowly. When I came to it, there was another car following me. I wanted to pass the semi, and it looked like a clear passage. Just when my front wheels were even with the semi's cab, my instinct made me step on the brake and slow down. And when the semi left my front end, my right front tire blew. I swerved to the right and I stopped on the shoulder right away. The car that was following me saw all that happened. It was a state patrolman. He came up to me and asked, "What happened?"

"I had a blowout!" I said. "Just when you saw me slow down, and the semi left me, I had that blowout." If I had continued on and passed, I would have been in front of that semi, a heavy, loaded semi, when I had the blowout. The patrolman asked me, "What made you do that?" "I do not know," I said. "Some instinct made me slow down, really put on the brake and slow down. Just as the semi passed my front wheel, I had that blowout and turned my car to the right." Luckily, I had a spare tire. The patrolman in his goodness took out his jack and turned his lights on. He waited while we jacked up the car and took off the wheel. Of course, I did all the work because the patrolman was in his uniform, and I did not want him to get muddy. But he was there all the time. He was eager to help. When we finished replacing the tire, he asked how far we were going. We said we were going close to thirty miles north of Rushville.

The patrolman then asked if we thought that our other tires were good. "If not, I will follow you all the way." He was that good, he was trying to help us. So, after we were through, he followed us to Hay Springs before he went on, making sure that we were okay.

»»→ • ←«««

I will tell you of another instance of this sort. One time in Colorado, the family went to a Fourth of July rodeo. I forget the town, but we were working near Fort Lupton at the time. I had bought a car in Denver, and we were going to this rodeo. We took in the activities, let the kids have fun, and bought candy and ice cream for them.

Highways in those times were narrow. On the way back, there was heavy traffic. I saw this heavy truck approaching, and I did not know what made me do it, but just as we came face to face with this truck, I turned the steering wheel halfway around to the right. We went off the side of the road. Just then, the left front tire blew out. If I had not done that, if I did not have the instinct to do that, we would have hit the side of the semi truck.

Occasions like this make me wonder, "Why? What made me do that?" As human beings, we do not see the future, what is going to happen in the next hour, or on the road. Those times I did the right thing at the right time to avoid accidents. And in all of these instances, the following night I could not sleep. That time I had my whole family with me—my wife, myself, and my small kids. We all could have perished there. But, I wonder, and I know that the Great Spirit protects us in times like this. I wonder, and I know that the Great Spirit in His mysterious ways protects us for a reason. That reason could be for us to seek out our lives, where we fit into this life, what we can do to help others, and help ourselves, to make this life worth living, to make it easier for ourselves and for others.

May the Great Spirit's love, and in His goodness, bless you. The Great Spirit will bless those people who may read this book. I pray He will implant in their hearts a love and compassion for the sick. If we can each in our own way, and according to our own means, be able to lend a hand to others, then we know that we live in the light of the Great Spirit.

Petaga Yuha Mani holding eagle fan and praying to the Great
Mystery, Medicine Bow Mountains.

Two *(Nunpa)*
ON BEING A MEDICINE MAN

Becoming a Medicine Man

Through the years, many people who are interested in what I do, and some who are skeptics for whatever reason, always ask me these questions: "What is it that makes you a medicine man? What is so special about it?" And sometimes they ask, "Is that the only thing you can do?" I always answer in the way that I am going to talk about now, about certain portions of my life as a medicine man.

I finally became a medicine man sixteen years after I was supposed to. I first had a sacred dream that I could not dispel. It was before me, it was in back of me, it was all around me. I could not live right; I could not sleep right; I could not eat right. It haunted me. I dreamed that I danced the Sundance and I was the only dancer.

In the Lakota way, you are supposed to act out a sacred vision. But I did not want it. In fact, I tried hard to avoid it. Why I did not want it is very simple to understand. I hated it because I was brought up in my early school days by the Jesuit missionaries. The missionaries infused in our minds that Indian ways, especially the doctoring and the Pipe ceremonies, were heathen ways. They said, "It is pagan worship and devil worship." Being young minds, we believed it. I believed it. That is why I had a difficult time for sixteen years, why I struggled to get away from my dream, to forget it.

This call of the medicine way of life was strong. It was close to me. It was in the meals that I ate. It was in my dreams, a constant reminder that I had to go that way. I even worked for the church for five years. But still that lingering thought stayed, wherever I was, whatever I was doing. Only when I was dead tired could I have a good night's sleep. I would walk and walk up in the hills way late at night and come in at midnight or later dead tired. I could then lay down on the bed, my shoes and everything on, and go to sleep. I spent months at a time working on ranches and farms in Nebraska, Wyoming, and Colorado. Just to forget, I worked like everything to tire myself physically so I could sleep well at night. I would seek out rough country or rough weather to dispel this feeling that was always close at hand, always close to me, whether I was doing ranch work or farm work, picking potatoes, working in a blizzard, going out to work when others would not want to. When I did irrigation work, I would go nineteen, twenty, twenty-one hours at a stretch, just so that I would be dog-tired when I went home. Sometimes, without even eating anything, I would just flop on the bed and go to sleep.

In trying to avoid becoming a medicine man, I even became part of the tribal council administration in the mid-

1960s. I was a tribal cop on three occasions, to get away from this haunting thing that was always close at hand. I wanted to forget it all. Sometimes, I even drank alcohol and got drunk to forget this sacred dream. But, when I sobered up it was still there, never to be blotted out.

Finally, I could not stand it anymore. So I thought to myself, "I will do this one thing that is part of the sacred dream, that I Sundance." In the Sundance dream, I was the lone dancer. That was the dream, and it was a hard dream. Sometimes I hear people say they had a sacred dream. Then, after telling me that their dream was dancing the Sundance, they would just go to a Sundance and dance it away. That tells me that their dream was not a sacred Sundance dream, because mine was so different from the way they dance nowadays. When I went to a Sundance, I would see six or seven dancers, and my dream did not fit that. I had to dance alone. Even this past year, in one Sundance there were perhaps a hundred dancers. But in the sacred dream I had, I was the lone dancer. Where could I do that?

So, the doing of the dream was a big problem. In my dream, only part of the Sundance arbor was whole and complete. The other part was just pine limbs stuck into the ground, and nowhere could I find a place like that. In the sacred dream I danced only one day, but I pierced in the morning, remained pierced all day, and all the while I danced I was crying. Because of this, it was doubly hard for me to fulfill this dream of mine. That is another reason why I kept postponing it for sixteen years.

Finally, on July 7, 1964, my family and a few other families got together and I fulfilled my sacred dream at a place known to us as Pte Woku (Feeding of the Buffalo). I thought I was going to dance and get it over with. We fixed that arbor just like in my dream. As in the dream, I pierced in the morning and I also cried the entire time that I danced. Nowadays, I go to Sundances and see people Sundancing. I do not see any of them crying. Mine was different; mine was hard to do. There was no play-acting; it was the real McCoy.

On that day, I stood pierced beneath the tree, and I was fighting, fighting to break free. There was a huge thunderstorm building in the west with very dark clouds, very close and low upon the horizon. Our people have a word for this kind of sky, *maka mani ukea* (close and on the ground it comes). There were some white clouds coming in between, some going up and some coming down. People were scared—they wanted to get away, since this was out in the rough country. The roads were hard to get through even when they were dry, and when it rained no car could come out of there. So, before it rained, they wanted to get back to the highway. Big drops of rain fell here and there, making a noise like hitting the ground. People were very anxious to leave. Some even got up and were walking toward their cars.

I called for my Pipe as in the dream, and when the Sundance helpers brought it to me I said the words that I dreamed to part the storm. I started praying. I pointed my Pipe to the advancing thunderstorm. You could hear the thunder, deep and heavy. It was close by, just about reaching us. I parted the thunderstorm in the center. Part of it went north, and part went south. The Sundance helpers watching the storm said that there were some eagles flying way up high, above the parted thunderhead. The part of the thunderhead that turned north went around by the White River country. It destroyed a lot of gardens and crops, and turned over a lot of outhouses, clear into the Kyle community area.

The thunderhead that turned south did the same kind of damage in Pine Ridge and beyond. There was much hail and high wind. Our beliefs of our culture tell us that when the Wakinyan (Thunder Beings) come over the land, they bring water; they want to shake up the earth, bring it to life, and they bring water to give the thirsty earth. But when you direct them elsewhere, they are *eyokipisni* (unhappy), they say *catkuta ukea* (from the back it comes), and they turn away and then reappear.

That is how it happened. In both directions, the thunderheads did a lot of damage, hailing out crops and tearing up trees. I continued my dancing. Only a few heavy, big raindrops fell here and there on us, but that was all. We continued with the dancing until late afternoon, when I broke free. When I broke free it seemed that peace had finally come to my spirit, that my physical being was appeased with the thought that the Great Spirit heard my prayer, and that the sacred dream that had tormented me for sixteen years was finally over. It seemed that now I would live without torment, that I would live a good life knowing that I had had an obligation, and that I had fulfilled it.

But it was not to be. I went deeper into spirituality. By reenacting this sacred dream and doing the Sundance, I had accepted that I would live traditionally the rest of my life and become a medicine man. In four consecutive summers, I would give a thanksgiving Pipefast in fulfillment of this sacred dream.

One thing that frightens me is that all the time that I danced I was crying. In the many years since then, even in Sundances that I directed—and I have directed eight consecutive Sundances at Little Eagle on the Standing Rock Reservation—I have never seen a dancer who danced and cried all the way through.

You see what a sacred dream really entails—it is hard to do and it frightens you. There is fear always, constantly with you and in you. It was there before me and every detail was in place. We fixed that arbor just as in the way of my dream. The part of the dream that I thought would be very hard was for me to cry all the way during the Sundance. But when I did go through with it that is exactly how it turned out to be. That dream and the reenacting of that sacred dream physically here on Mother Earth became one. This is how the power becomes real in a medicine man.

I recall now, after these many years, how tormented a period I came through, suffering physically. I should add spiritually, too, because in avoiding my dream, I did not even want to pray. It was so very real that, even now, it makes me feel how small I am, how humble I am. In order to advance in the presence of the Great Spirit, one has to be humble.

Looking back over the years, I know what sacred means: it is something that we have to do to become worthy physically and spiritually in order to fulfill some sacred thing. That Sundance dream was not the only sacred dream I have had. I have had many sacred visions, and my name—Petaga Yuha Mani (He Walks with Hot Coals)—is derived from one of the visions I had.

The first summer, in 1958, that I went on a fast I had a vision. That vision was on the third day—I was standing in the heat of the summer day, heat so strong and heavy. I did not know what the temperature was and I did not ask. I let it be how it was. So, standing there on the third day, weary, tired, thirsty, hungry, I held my Pipe up and it would gradually come down, and I tried hard to put it back up. And it would gradually come down, and I tried hard to put it back up again.

You see, Wakan Tanka made me as I am. And when I want to serve, I give it all that I have. So, I did not stand there with the Pipe resting on my stomach, or my elbows resting on my stomach. I held that Pipe up as high as I could and tried to hold it up hours and hours at a time, because I wanted the Great Spirit to bless this Pipe. By blessing this Pipe I wanted Him to bless me too, so that this Pipe and me would be like one; that whatever I did with this sacred Pipe, the Great Spirit would listen. Many times throughout my life I asked the Great Spirit to do something that is almost impossible, but being humble, being

>>>→ • ←<<<

lowly, feeling unworthy, He grants me what I ask of Him. This is what makes me a medicine man.

So, I was standing there like that, raising the Pipe up there, and singing a sacred song. And when the Pipe was coming down, I noticed a man who was standing and facing the other way. In my vision, on the left side of the Pipe at a distance perhaps twenty, twenty-five yards out there, this man turned right and crossed over the Pipe. And when he did, there was a huge fire burning where he was going. He stopped short of the fire, knelt down, and took some sticks aside. He reached underneath and raked forth some hot coals. Then he cupped his hands, took a double heaping handful of hot coals, and he started to get up. He turned the other way, went very slowly around the fire, and then everything, the scene that I was seeing, disappeared. This was the vision.

When I came back from the fast I related what I had seen on that third day to the medicine man who was taking care of me. He did not know what to make of it, and he said, "This is meant for you alone. It is not meant for me to tell you; this is meant for you alone, and you will know yourself what it means."

About a year afterward, a man came to our home. He said, "My father is very sick; I want you to come and doctor him. I was to bring you a Pipe, but knew that if I brought that Pipe and you were not here, that would be a sure sign that my father is in a bad way. So, in order to be sure, I came alone. When you get there I will offer you that Pipe."

When I came close to the dwelling I could tell that they were smudging the inside of the house because I saw smoke coming out of the open doorway. I went in, and to my left was a cookstove with a burning fire. This was in the afternoon, and there was a kettle of water that was steaming. And when I went in, the man who had come after me took a chair and placed it in front of his father's bed, so I sat down facing the sick man.

The son came around in the back with the Pipe and offered me the Pipe. He lit the Pipe for me. I sat there, offering the Pipe to the Four Directions, and up above, and down to the earth. I sat there smoking, and I could feel the heavy gaze of someone looking at me. While I was smoking, I opened my eyes and looked at the old man. He was really staring at me, and I could tell there was concern in his eyes. I could read his thoughts. He was thinking, "What is this son of a bitch trying to do? Does this son of a bitch think that he can cure me?" He had that on his mind. Because I had the sacred Pipe in my hand, I was able to see his thoughts. I continued smoking until I was through.

In the group of people gathered there, there was one person, a close friend of mine who knows my altar, who knows the way I do things, the way I do doctoring. I called him over. "Get some cedar," I said, "and get a sweetgrass braid and crumble it together; mix it up. Hold it in your hand, and when I nod to you, come and help me." He went and got these things together. I got up and I walked as in the vision that I had seen. I walked slowly to that fire, to that stove—it was a wood kitchen stove with the firebox door in front. I opened it, and there was a large amount of hot coals there. I reached in there and raked forth hot coals like what I had seen in the vision, and took two heaping handfuls. Then I went slowly, turned around, and came back to where I was sitting. I nodded to my helper. He rushed forth and put the cedar and the crumpled sweetgrass onto the hot coals. This is how I smudged that sick old man, and how he was healed.

Constitution of a Medicine Man

I will try to explain what a medicine man is, what makes him a medicine man. In my wanderings here and there as a medicine man, I have talked of it, but I have never given a full account of what really constitutes a medicine man.

A medicine man first has to be honest with himself. He has to be truthful, and he has to be humble. Wakan Tanka works in many strange and mysterious ways. He calls upon the weakest to do a great thing. He calls upon the lowly, the poor man, to do His handiwork, that of curing human beings who are sick.

Humility is such a great thing, one of the essential things. We medicine men do not jump to the center. We do not raise our hands and say, "Here! Here! Here I am!" We stay in the background. A true medicine man does not walk the streets showing himself. He stays out where he lives. Somebody that needs a medicine man will go search for him and find him there. This is the true way of a medicine man.

>>>→ • ←<<<

These medicine men that go from state to state in search of the things that they want to do are not medicine men at all. It makes me think back over the years. I saw an old movie one time. Somewhere in the West, there was this so-called medicine man in sort of a sheep wagon, drawn by a team of horses, with his medicine advertisement written on the side. One of the things I remember well was "A sure cure for all ills and pains." He had medicine comprised of snake oil, crushed grasshoppers, and all of that. Everywhere we still have these kinds of medicine men. They go from state to state proclaiming their power, that they are able to do this and that. I often wonder: Do these same medicine men have traces of Indian in them? Do they have in their hip pocket a bottle of snake oil or crushed grasshoppers, ants, or whatever?

So, a true medicine man has to be humble. He has to stay where he lives. He has to be known where he lives. He has to practice whatever he does in his own community. Those who live around him go to him and seek his help. This is the kind of medicine man I am talking about, not the moving kind, the fly-by-night sort of medicine man.

A true medicine man lives a simple life. He lives without a lot of fancy pleasures, and this makes him stronger. When I was younger, I made myself suffer. I brought suffering upon myself. Now, I look at other people in different areas, like the church people, ministers, and priests. I have watched and worked with many. You see, for five years, I worked for the church when I was trying to get away from becoming a medicine man. I saw some church people who did likewise. They omit pleasures like smoking cigarettes and eating candy. These are some of the common easy things to avoid, but in a sense, it adds up to a great deal.

I have been called to Hawaii on two occasions. The first time I went to Maui; the second time I went to Oahu. The second time I went there, a person called and invited me to his home. He was sitting there on a rug. He was barefooted and shaggy, and he had a full, long beard. He said he was a holy man. There was a girl sitting on his left, there was a girl sitting on his right, and he was very talkative. He said, "I am a holy man. I had a vision, a great vision. I saw God, and He spoke to me." As he was saying this, he was smoking weed, smoking marijuana. He took a couple of puffs and gave it to the girl on his left. She took two puffs and gave it to the other girl. That made me mad.

I told him, "Listen you, if you spoke to God, you would leave the pleasures of this world alone, you would not even notice them. You would get away from them. You would, perhaps, go live up in the mountains, go without food all day long, fast from drinking water, instead of sitting there smoking pot with girls on each side of you.... You make me sick. You and your kind make me sick. It is the thing that you are smoking that makes you hallucinate. You are make-believe."

I got up and walked away. He called me back, and I said, "No! You live in another world, in a dopey world. I will have nothing to do with you!"

So, too, in the medicine man world, the real one, the real medicine man is not fat. He might be a sorry-looking guy. He is thin, he might be weak physically, but his spirit is very strong. This constitutes a medicine man. Those who go from state to state, carrying their snake oil and crushed grasshoppers, these kinds of medicine men go after money. They live good but their work is not always beneficial; it does not help the people. Why they do this is hard to understand. What they do reflects on everyone. It reflects on me, and I hate for people to think that I might be that way too.

A medicine man does not fight. He does not raise his voice in anger. He does not raise his fist in anger. He does not even own a rifle. But the Tunkasilas (the Spirits, or Grandfathers) that watch over him really do take care of him. I never experienced anybody coming up to me and slapping me or hitting me. If that ever happened, the Tunkasilas will do the revenge for me, even though I do not want them to. Anybody having bad feelings toward me gets his payback in terms of bad luck or misfortune, so to speak. This happens over and over again. My wife understands this very well; she sees it. I do not like it; I do not foster this. I would let things ride as they are, but it happens that I am not saying everybody has to be good to me. No, that is not the way. We are human and we have our bad feelings. I, too, have bad feelings. Sometimes my mind is so warped, you know, with watching the alcohol-related suffering that goes on, things that happen from alcohol, especially when I see a baby pass from this life through alcohol-related things. Some hurt,

>>>→ • ←<<<

some anger, comes into my being. Sometimes that bad feeling cannot be controlled.

I say to people in order to satisfy them that being a medicine man is the hardest thing a person can do because we did not go to medical school. Myself, I am very ignorant. I am lowly, I am humble. But still I can doctor people for mental problems, heart conditions, stomach conditions, ulcers, diabetes, and arthritis. I have doctored people with phobias and they got well. I have doctored people with eye problems and they got well. So, a medicine man is ignorant, because he has not gone through many books of teachings and instructions and medical classes. Yet, with the power of the Great Spirit and the dreams that he has, supernatural things and the physical world unite as one to give him a power.

A medicine man can pass his power on to his sons. I have four grandfathers in this world that we are in. One grandfather married into the Arapahoe tribe, one grandfather married into the Cheyenne tribe, and one grandfather married into the Oglalas. We are formerly from the Standing Rock Reservation. Hunkpapa (one of the seven bands of the Tetons), Sitting Bull's band, is where we come from. But one of my grandfathers married into the Oglalas, and that is how we are here. One grandfather left and never came back. No one knows where he went. Maybe he was killed somewhere. No one knows. There is no history of it.

So, being a medicine man is hereditary. All four grandfathers of mine were medicine men. My father was a medicine man, and he quit being a medicine man and joined the church. That is how he left this world; he died that way. I worked for the church at one time for five years, and I left the church and became a medicine man. Generation after generation, we pass on the heredity of medicine men. Of my two sons who are following me, one of them will become a medicine man when I leave this world.

On the other hand, being a Lakota chief is not hereditary. A chief must earn his status. The Oglalas nowadays, especially under this new tribal council way, take so many cut-acrosses. In one family, I will not mention the name, the first chief could not pass it on through the clan, but that is what is happening today. They call themselves chiefs but they have no real status. Out on the traditional reservation, here in the backwoods so to speak, we do not look to that family as being chiefs.

Becoming a chief has to be earned from childhood. There are many, many virtues that have to be shown and learned, such as generosity, kindness, having courage, having respect for oneself and for others, being wise, and being a leader. A leader must be a role model. A leader must have the trust of the people that he is leading. How can they follow him if they do not trust him?

I would say that most of the tribe here does not feel that we have a chief, because that world is gone. We have young men who went to war, but that too is not of the same status as compared with warriors of long ago. A warrior of that age and a soldier of today are both courageous, they have both done brave deeds, they have both won honors.

>>>→ • ←<<<

But, being a soldier today means that they have to pledge allegiance to the United States flag. There you have it. They are not working for the tribe; they are working for another nation. So, in that sense, they are warriors under another flag. They are not warriors under a tribal flag. We have to understand these things.

Becoming a chief is not hereditary, but a medicine man can give his powers to the next generation. This is tradition. This is the heritage that we have, and nothing can change it. We can fool around like many do in many things, like with the Sundance and the sweat lodges, but the Great Spirit will either bless or will not bless what we do—that is the main thing to think about.

In my work, the first thing I think about when people want my help is: Do they really believe in this? In the years that I have worked as a medicine man, I have seen people come to a medicine man only when they need one, and in between, they do not care for him. Only when he is needed, he is taken off that shelf, and they use him and then put him away. But there are also people that keep you in mind. They know what you are, they respect you, and that makes you feel good. They know that you are a person too. They know that you are hungry, that you get tired, just like any other human being.

A medicine man will go all out like I do, and do all he can to provide the services asked of him by the people, such as funerals, marriages, blessings, namings, even prayers. My wife knows; many times on these marches that we have been doing, I would get home very tired, not from the walking, but from the great impact of the meaning of the marches, such as DADD (Dads Against Drunk Driving). There are just a handful of us marching the roads against drunk driving. How many dads are there on the reservation? Are all the rest of them alcohol users? Maybe some of them are drunk drivers themselves. Do they not love their children in the way they should love their children, to go out there on the road and walk for the sake of their children?

These things go through my mind. Are our children going to grow up to be young men and women and have this problem that we have in front of us, still here with us, or maybe much worse? So, during a march, when I pray on the road, and when I sing sacred songs on the road, it drains a heck of a lot of energy from me. When I get home, I am so tired—spiritually, not physically. I am not tired because of the walking, but from the prayers that I say imploring the Great Spirit to help us.

If I could choose to live like an ordinary person, most certainly I would grab that chance, because a medicine man is not a happy man. The only time that he is happy is when he knows he has cured a patient, when he knows that he has cured a sickness. That in itself is reward enough. A true medicine man never asks for any fees. He lives as lowly as possible. When you see one, you will know he is a true medicine man because he is not of this world. He does not go to pow-wows, he does not take pleasure in life; he does not go to circuses, rodeos, or anything. He stays at home. It is a lonely life. That is one of the great sacrifices he has to make.

I wonder how many young bucks today qualify to become medicine men. They think of it in terms of glory. It is not glorious. That is not how I see it—it requires many sacrifices, such as fasting.

Through my years of being a medicine man, I have been called to work in many states, including Hawaii, Nebraska, Wyoming, Colorado, Montana, North Dakota, South Dakota, and in Rosebud country, Lower Brulé, and many other reservations. Above all, I work in my own community. A medicine man is not choosy; he goes where he is wanted. He is not a member of any organization. He is a spiritual worker. He can go anywhere where he is wanted and work with people who want to use him or need him. So, it is not a glory thing and it is nothing to brag about. The more years that you tie yourself to it, the more that you want to get away from it. It is a lifelong thing—you are a medicine man until your dying breath.

A Doctoring Trip to Hawaii

The first time I went to Hawaii, I went to Maui. When I was ready to go home, people just did not want me to leave. They even suggested I stay and make my home there. I told them that South Dakota is my home and where I was born, and that I would like to return to the people I know, the people who are part of me.

As I said before, a medicine man cannot be choosy. He goes where he is called. And the second time I went to Hawaii in March 1974 was one such instance. I did not want to go back because of the difficult time I had coming away from there the first time. I got a phone call telling me that I had a ticket to Hawaii waiting for me in Rapid City, but I did not want to go. I was just about to forget it when I received a letter from the people who had sent the ticket, explaining why they wanted me there. The mother of the family that sent for me is my niece. She is married to a person who was in the Air Force and he was stationed in Oahu. They have two daughters and one son. The son is the youngest. He was six years old at the time. In the letter, they explained that their son was very listless, very sick, that he acted like an old man. He had lost interest in everything, including his friends, and even playing. In a word, they wanted me to doctor him.

One part of the boy's father's family history is unusual. Little John, the sick boy, was the only son. Little John's father was the only son in his family, and in the grandfather's family, the grandfather was an only son. This was probably going through the minds of the family, that John was an only son of an only son of an only son.

When I read that letter, I packed up my suitcase and I started walking toward the highway from where I was living at Mission Flat. There was fresh snowfall and the day was warm. Everywhere the snow was melting, creating runoff. You could not walk anywhere without splashing, so I did not go by the road; I took a cut-across through the fields to reach Highway 18. In the Calico community, they call this place Mission Flat. I reached the highway and I started walking.

There I was hitchhiking to Rapid City, carrying my suitcase. I was walking on this flat, and just about the time I was going to go down a hill, I heard a car slow down, right where our land touches the highway. I did not even look back. The car slowed down and stopped, and then it came on beside me. Someone held the door open. "Get in, Uncle Pete," he said, so I got in. It was a pickup so I threw the suitcase in the back and I got in the front. It was my nephew, Eddie Whitewolf, and one of his friends.

Eddie asked me, "Where are you going?" This is a very common question around our area. People always see me walking the highway. I am usually going to Oglala, Pine Ridge, or somewhere nearby for a ceremony or whatever. Since I was carrying my suitcase, he knew I was going to a ceremony. So I told him I was going to Hawaii.

He thought I was joking, and said, "and walking too," and the two looked at each other. They did not believe me. "Really," he said, "where are you going?" "Hawaii," I said. "My gosh, let us turn around and go back," said Eddie. They lived just off the highway. "Let us turn around and go back and have some coffee, and then we will take you to Hawaii." They still thought I was joking.

We turned around and went back to my nephew's house. They fried some hamburger and eggs and made some coffee. They invited me to eat and I did. I had my mind on Hawaii and the sick young boy. While we were eating, my nephew asked me, "Uncle, where are you really going?" "I told you, I am going to Hawaii. I have a ticket waiting in Rapid City," I said.

"Oh! Now we believe you," he said. "We will take you to Rapid City. We will take you to the airport and see when you can take off." I was glad of that. I got a ride all the way into Rapid City, which is about 160 miles away.

We drove to Rapid City that afternoon and went straight to the airport. Eddie inquired for me if I had a ticket there. The agent looked through the computer, and sure enough, I had a ticket with an open date. They said the next flight was not until the next day, so we drove back to town and got a motel room. We had supper and went to bed. The next morning we got ready, and by noon we reached the airport. They did see me off. I guess when they did see me off, they really, firmly believed that I was telling the truth. Believe it or not, this is what actually happened. This is the way the sacred Pipe works. All you need to do is have faith in it, strong and deep enough that you can take off on foot, depending on nothing else, asking for no favors from anyone, but just take off and the sacred Pipe will take care of you.

Hawaii is a paradise on earth sort of thing. Rich people go there to pass the time of day, to enjoy the weather, the fruits, whatever Hawaii has to offer. "Aloha" is the going word. When visitors from the mainland arrive there, they are given a lei, a string of beautiful flowers placed over the neck. I arrived in Hawaii after 11 p.m. their time. As is always my custom, whenever I am deplaning, debussing, or whatever, I keep my seat until everybody has stood in line and left. I am always the last one to get in line and follow the crowd. The other travelers on my plane all got one lei. When it came my turn, I had one upon another. I had seven leis around my neck. Oh, these people I was flying with, they really looked at me. They thought I was a freak or something. But anyway, that is what happened.

The family met me at the airport and took me home. They knew I was tired. We had a quick meal and went to bed. The next morning, we visited and they told me about the problem. Little John was in the army hospital for observation. From the x-rays, the doctors thought he was suffering from leakage of the heart. Surgery would be required to see if that was the problem. On the twenty-fourth of the month, Little John was to go to the army hospital for heart surgery.

So, they gave me a day of rest and I explained to them what I was going to do. We were going to go into a ceremony. I asked if they could bring Little John home for a ceremony and they said they could. I explained the essential things, that when they pray they should really mean every word that they used in their prayer and it should be a positive prayer. I also told them how to prepare for a ceremony. They needed to get colored flags, tobacco pouches, and food, because no ceremony is complete without a feast. Whether that feast entails just Kool-Aid and sandwiches, it is still called a feast. Every ceremony has to be followed by a feast. All of this is included in the ceremony; what you put out is perhaps what you get.

That night we went into a ceremony. Friends of the family gathered there with them to help out. They brought whatever they wished to the feast. And they came to help pray. In the ceremony, I told the parents that there was leakage of the heart, that there was a hole in Little John's heart. I told them I would fix this up and it would not trouble him anymore. The way I explained it was that I am only an instrument of Wakan Tanka, the Great Spirit. I said that I was only a part of the doctoring, and the Great Spirit and the spirits that were with me as helpers would do the doctoring. In this way, x-rays taken afterward would not show that the little boy had leakage of the heart.

I took a small drum with me that I carried in a suitcase to use in the ceremony. After the ceremony, we visited with the other people. They were glad to see me and were enthused about the ceremony and the singing. That was the first time a lot of them ever smoked from the Pipe. I told them, "When you smoke the Pipe, the smoke represents the breath of the Great Spirit. So what you pray for, either to help somebody else or to help yourself, your prayer should be on your mind while you are smoking the sacred Pipe."

Cansasa, Indian tobacco, is a very different sort of a tobacco. They work together, the cansasa and the Peace Pipe. I have seen people who use Bull Durham in their Peace Pipe, but I do not go for that. That was not the way when the Peace Pipe was brought to the Lakota people. The original way was the cansasa, and that is how it should be. It is traditional when you use cansasa in a Pipe. Well, the first time they smoked it after the ceremony was completed, they all liked the flavor of the cansasa in the Pipe, and they were really enthused by all of this.

The following morning was the time the family was to take the young boy to the army hospital. I used to remember the names of that hospital and the important places on Oahu, Maui, and elsewhere too, but it has been many years since then. I should have written their names down but I did not. I lived each day as it presented itself. I had never intended that someday I would try to recall the names of places that I visited. So, I no longer recall those names.

I do remember that the hospital was situated on a hillside and all the buildings were pink. It was very beautiful. We took Little John there. That day the boy was to be given another examination, pre-surgery, I think it is called. When they examined him, the x-ray films came out negative and the doctors could not believe it. They took the old film and compared the two. Looking at them, the two were completely different. The old one showed leakage of the heart and the new one showed nothing. Nothing was wrong. Little John went through a physical again, the x-ray part. But still it came out as before. There was nothing wrong with the boy. They kept him overnight, and the following morning they x-rayed him again, for the third time. He was free from leakage of the heart. So, he was released. We went after him and took him home.

From the time of the ceremony up to the time that we brought him back from the hospital, there was a great deal of difference in Little John's attitude. His listlessness was gone. He had acted like an old man when I first saw him. He was sitting there with a bowed head, like he had given up all hope. That was gone. He was lively, he was smiling. He was like his old self.

At the supper table, when we were through eating, I talked to the father and the mother. The kids had finished eating and were in another room, so they did not hear. I said, "This does not mean that Little John is completely well. No, what the spirit helpers did was cover up that leakage. They covered it up so the x-ray could not show how it was before. But when I get back to South Dakota, and when the snow falls on the country where I come from, then Little John will be completely well. But from now until the first snow in South Dakota you must never punish this boy, no matter what he does. Never spank him, never scold him. He is going to be a rascal. He is going to make you feel that anger come to you. But remember, this is the consequence you must face. If you do not scold him, if you do not whip him, he will become completely well by the first snowfall in South Dakota."

The next morning, Little John was up on the roof. Oh heck, it could get any mother frustrated. It could get any father red in the face. But they coaxed him down. Before the day was over, he broke the back windshield of their station wagon. By gosh, he was a rascal, climbing trees like a monkey. My visit was in March, so all through that spring and summer they had a mischievous little son who was everywhere, like Dennis the Menace in the cartoon. It was that way for the length of time just as the spirits said it would be. But that was the consequence of this healing.

Little John was into everything. He would break dishes and everything else. I guess he was worse than Dennis the

Menace. It seems like he was wise talking too and he had things to say that taunted his parents. When I left, he was roughing it up, making misery for everybody. But he was healthy. He was putting food away, he was sleeping good, and he was doing somersaults and everything that you would think a person with leakage of the heart would not go through. He was going to show his parents that Indian religion, Indian healing, works.

I got letters from Little John's mother after the following winter, saying that he was periodically examined at the army hospital, but no trace of this leakage of the heart ever appeared again. He is a young man now, and he has a family and a job.

When I hear of things like this, the result of something I did, that I was a part of the instrument of the working of the Great Spirit and the sacred Pipe, it makes me all that much more humble. And I wonder sometimes, how does it work? I do not know myself. But it does work, and Indian people live in it and by it. Indian people have problems, but I am sure that they are very trivial compared to our everyday problems if we were not in this so-called Indian religion.

Everything has a balance in this world—everything! There is a balance in this healing. It is not always the sort that I mentioned here. There are other consequences that could follow in the wake of a healing. So, here again I will say that Indian religion is unique. It is a religion different from all other religions. In this religion, we must have faith. That is the going word.

I have heard people say they go to this and that doctor and they cannot be cured, and that they will try this and that. There is no faith in such thinking, such as "I will try this Indian medicine way." More often than not, this "trying thing" does not work. You have to believe in it. It does not mean you have to believe to be a member of something. Do you believe in a pill, in an aspirin, to cure your headache? You know it is going to cure your headache. There you have that belief, a faith about something that will make you whole, that will cure you.

This is how Indian religion works. Indian religion is unique; it is something that Wakan Tanka gave to us. We do not need x-rays, modern techniques, and the latest in modern powerful drugs to cure our ills. Instead, we ask the Great Spirit, the Creator of all things, to make us whole, to cure us. His word is medicine. His word is healing. We are truly the children of the Great Spirit because He watches over us, He takes care of us, and I know He loves us.

Praying at Difficult Times

In every person's life, there comes a time when they reach their prime. It may happen at any age, when they get to be the strongest, or when they get to be the heaviest. This sort of thing happened to me.

In the summer of 1969, I conducted two Sundances, one at Spring Creek on the Rosebud Reservation and one right here on the Pine Ridge Indian Reservation. My weight was 206 pounds and I was healthy and strong. In the early winter of that year, in January, we were living in a cabin below a hill. The main hill runs sort of southwest to north-east. There is a branch in the ridge that reaches out to the right, or toward the east. It was below this point that my wife and I had a little cabin. There was deep snow on the ground, and prior to this time I was talking to my oldest brother Joe.

He was telling me about prayer. He said, "The Great Spirit is everywhere. He is in the room with you. He sees and knows what you are doing. Because He is always near, He knows your every action, your every deed. We should always be aware that the Great Spirit is always nearby, sometimes to help us, sometimes to just watch over us, sometimes to see what goes on in our minds."

My brother told me, "When the Great Spirit is nearest to you, that is the time to talk to Him. When the going is rough and tough, when trials of life are hardest to meet, that is the time to talk to the Great Spirit. I do not care where it is, because that is the time He is closest to you."

I always remember what else my brother said: "No matter where you are...when you are lying underneath a car, many times your wrench slips, you hit your hand on the frame or some part of the car, you go to cussing around...or riding along on horseback, something spooks the horse and you go to bucking, and when something does not go the way it should. I do not care where you are, whatever you are doing; He is there beside you. When misery or problems assail you and the going is tough, that is the time to pray to Him. That is the time to talk to Him, because that is the time He is closest to you."

>>>→ • ←<<<

One day I was thinking of what my brother told me. That night we were without food. We had very little. We were out of coffee, sugar, and some essential things, and we practically went to bed hungry. I was thinking about what my brother was saying, "When the going is tough, that is the time you should talk to Him." I intended to go up on a hill to pray. So, I waited.

Later that night my wife went to sleep. Way past midnight, I got up. I started putting on my shoes and my overshoes because there was a strong wind blowing outside and the snow was ten or eleven inches deep and the drifts were even deeper. When I was putting on my jacket, my wife got up and asked me what I was doing. I told her, "You know what my brother was telling us one time, that when the going was tough that we should talk to the Great Spirit. Because when it is the toughest, that is the time He is closest to you." She said she remembered. "So, I am going up the hill, up to the very top, against the wind, and pray." She said, "All right, don't be gone long. Do not stay up there too long."

I opened the firebox to the heating stove, put a few more logs in it, and then I went outside. I took the outhouse path, which was cleared, and from there on was deep snow. It was in high drifts in some places. I was headed for the point of the branch that fingers out toward the east. I had a difficult time climbing up to that point. I was among pine trees, so the going was all right. There were only gusts of wind and the swirling of snow. I slowly followed the ridge way. As I have said, in every person's life there comes a time when he is in his prime of life. I was at that point, 206 pounds, strong and heavy. I followed that ridge way slowly, going around boulders. Sometimes, I had to turn around and face downwind because the wind was getting stronger as I ascended to the top. I would catch my breath and then turn and go again. Finally, I came to the top.

After I reached the top, I knew what my brother Joe was talking about, when the going is toughest. There I was, at a point when the going was toughest. I came from a home that was close to minus in food. I was all alone up there on the hill; it was way past midnight and the rest of the world was asleep. Strong gusts of wind staggered me. But I braced myself, and took out my Pipe, facing the wind. I remember what I said. "I want many more like this (*Lena ota makuye*)." I never thought what those two or three words meant. The meanings are so numerous. It means suffering; it means problems, problems that come in many forms, in many ways, sometimes every day, and far into the night. So, I prayed up there, and I remember those words, "Lena ota makuye."

I finished my prayer. I sat down and tried to light that Pipe, but could not. There was no lighter or match that could hold the flame long enough to puff on that Pipe, no matter what effort I put into it. So, I retreated downhill. I came around a boulder; I stopped there and wondered if I should try there. All along that finger of ridge pointing toward the east, I tried several places to light that Pipe, but I could not light it. In my mind, I wanted to be alone because I was talking to the Great Spirit. Any effort that I put into lighting that Pipe would not work. When I tried to light the Pipe, the flame would just flicker and go out. So, I went directly home, opened the firebox, got a coal and placed it on the bowl, and I went back up to that point on the ridge from where I had come down.

I went back up there, sat in the snow, and smoked my Pipe. I felt at peace. It is hard to explain. I finished smoking the Pipe and I started downhill again. It must have been easily two o'clock. By that time my going back and forth made a trail, so going back down the last time was easier.

I got back inside the cabin, which was warm and good, and cleaned my pipe and put it away. I sat in a chair and relaxed. We had a dog named Lassie, a big shepherd dog. She would not bark at us or at anyone she knew who came to visit us, but she would bark at something or someone that she had not seen coming to our place before. She started growling and barking. My wife said, "There is someone coming." Sure enough, even though it was very late, I heard footsteps in the snow, kind of squeaky like. Pretty soon, there was a knock on the door. I went and opened it and I had five visitors: John Fire Lame Deer, and Richard Erdoes, and his wife and two sons.

My visitors had traveled to the Black Hills and made several stops. They had car trouble coming back, but their intent was to see me before they left on their trip back to the Rosebud country. At that time, Richard Erdoes was in the process of writing a book.[8] He made a short tape, and

I spoke on the tape. I do not recall what was said, but before he left, Richard reached in his pocket and gave me twenty dollars.

Wakan Tanka answers our prayers in an out-of-time, out-of-the-way manner. I did not ask for help. All I said was "I want many more like this," meaning the place where I am, where it is the hardest to get to, where the trials seem the hardest, where the problem is the heaviest, where tears usually come. That is the time the Great Spirit is closest, but He is always near us. I did not expect anything like this; money was the farthest thing from my mind. Because of this, I know what my brother Joe said is true.

Once again, I would like to say a little bit about my home, the trailer camp. I doubt if anybody can live there in this kind of weather. It started to snow earlier this evening and the wind chill factor over the past week is 50 to 70 below zero. My home is one of these trailers that in the 1960s they hitched to a car and trailed along the highways. It is a narrow thing, and 30 feet long. But that is where I live. I am only glad to have a home.

This morning and yesterday morning, I went back to the trailer camp because I have a dog still living there and I had to feed it. I have my sweat lodge close by, all fenced up, with the wind blowing the covers away. But the sweat lodge rocks are there. The prayers of people, the prayers that I say are there; they echo from those very rocks. Those same rocks were red hot at one time, this past summer and the summer before. And it is there for part of a time period that Wakan Tanka was close to us and helped us. And there, young men and young women have fasted at my sweat lodge. Some have used the sweat lodge, and some have gone out in the hills on Hanbleceya (Pipefast).

The place where I live is all hills; the terrain is rough. There are many ideal places where a person can Hanbleceya. That is where I live. I know that is where the good things will grow. If only we will see, even through the snow and the cold, the good things that Wakan Tanka has given us. Even though it is cold, even though there is snow, even though we suffer, even though we are hungry, even though our lives seem miserable, far beyond that, He is always close by. In the depths of our troubles is the goodness of the Great Spirit. Always remember that the time to pray is when the going is rough, because that is the time He is closest to you. And if you live as humbly as I do, you can be sure that the Great Spirit dwells there also.

Petaga Yuha Mani, 1990.

Three *(Yamni)*
STORIES & LESSONS

Lakota Creation—"We Are Little Brother to the Buffalo"

This is the story of how the buffalo and the Lakota became brothers. Long ago, so the legend goes, there was grass above the waist in the draws in these rolling plains. The grass was that tall, leaning over one way or the other. It was bountiful, and wherever there was a herd of buffalo, there were always bulls. There was the head bull, and the younger ones. The bulls encircled the grazing buffalo herd because there would be calves among them, yearlings and smaller ones. In that time, bears and wolves were plentiful on the plains. These bears and wolves would prey on the weak and old buffalo. For protection, the leaders in the buffalo herd encircled the other buffalo and they would face out.

This legend tells us that an old buffalo bull was standing there on the plains. It was a cold and windy day. Somewhere he heard a voice crying. The voice said four things: "I am cold. I am hungry. I am weak. I am thirsty." The old buffalo bull was listening. The power of the myste-

rious Wakan Tanka to instill into the mind of this old buffalo bull to think kindly is amazing. Besides, the old bull was a
fighter; he knew many years of battle with the other bulls.
He was a proud leader. But, the Great Spirit instilled into
this buffalo the thought that what he was hearing, what he
understood, was that someone was cold, hungry, weak, and
thirsty. The buffalo bull sought the direction in which the
voice was coming. But it was hard to discern because the
wind was blowing. He went down close to the earth, and
tried to follow the sound, that weeping, that crying.

In the course of time, he came to a blood clot. It was
this blood clot that was crying, "I am cold. I am hungry. I am
weak. I am thirsty." The old buffalo bull sniffed at it and he
looked very closely. That blood clot was the Lakota people,
the Red Man. It was there that the Great Spirit inspired in
this buffalo that he would give everything of himself, his
whole being, and even his spirit, to this one in need.

So, the buffalo bull said to this crying individual, "I
will be your big brother, I will give you all that I am. Look at
me, I am strong. I am not weak, I am strong. I went through
all these years fighting my battles, winning out. I bear the
scars of battle. But I am victorious and I am to this point in
life a leader in the herd, so I am not weak. Look about you.
All over creation is my feed. I can eat here. I can eat there. I
can eat everywhere, so I am never hungry. Look at me.

"Look at me. Look at my mane. The fore part of my
being is all fur. When the blizzard winds blow, I walk facing
the blowing wind, and can eat the grass on the way. And
when I stand still I face the wind because the fore part of my

being is all fur, and I am never cold. So, I will make you my little brother. We will be like one; we will be together. You can have my hide to live in. You can have my flesh to eat so you will not be hungry. You will be like me. When you do these things, you will be strong."

So, there, at that instant, that moment, the buffalo and the Lakota became brothers. That is why the Lakota use every part of the buffalo that they kill. Not one single part of it is wasted or thrown away. In many instances, the Lakota used buffalo for curing of any sickness. The part of the meat on the hump of the buffalo is held sacred by the Lakota. We use that mixed with medicine.

If this world continued in the fashion before the white man came, we would still be a lovely, beautiful people. There would be buffalo on the land. There would be deer and all kinds of animals, along with the Lakota people. They call it the "wild, wild West." It was paradise before the white man. It was only wild after the white man came, because they shot at random, at anything that moved. They did away with the buffalo and with all the wild game; only a few animals remain. The buffalo that we know are in the state parks and just recently, some people have buffalo ranches. That is the greed of the white man. What the Creator made in this Western Hemisphere was meant for the Native people, but the white man came and took it all.

Long before the advent of the white man with his medical profession, medical techniques reached the Indian country. We Lakota people have long performed blood transfusions. When the warriors would go out on a hunt,

>>>—→ • ←—<<<
73

they would bring back buffalo blood. If there was a very sick person who was just hide and bones, the medicine man would give that person a drink of buffalo blood. The medicine man would take a spoonful of the buffalo's live blood, the warm live blood, and give it to the sick.

Three years ago, on the Standing Rock Reservation where we used to conduct the Sundances, they were butchering a buffalo, and I asked to go along. My son, Peter Catches, came along too. I purposely took a cup with me. When they started butchering, when they had it open, I reached under the *taniga* (tripe) and got a cupful of buffalo blood and I drank it. Everybody was startled. They really looked at me. Peter came over and said, "Dad, get me some." So, when I drank it up I reached over, got a cupful and handed it to him. He drank it too. This is what the Native Americans did long ago. Now we see this as a blood transfusion. When the buffalo gave his all to the Lakota people, that is what he meant. He is life giving. The buffalo gave everything around him to his younger brother so that he can be strong, so that he can continue to live in this world.

Wintercount

In the books that you read about our people, the Lakota, we are always referred to as savages. The books say of us that we are pagan worshippers, and that we are heathens. But from the beginning of time, we have always been inspired by the Great Spirit, as we are even today. We have to search to find out why we are here in this world. I will now touch on a tale of long ago. It has to do with a buffalo hunt, a warrior, and his hunting pony.

Our people are nomadic; we traveled around the Ka Sapa (Black Hills). Being that the buffalo sacrifices his whole life to help his younger brother, the Lakota people stayed close to buffalo herds. Buffaloes numbered in the millions and millions. You did not have to look for them. All you had to do was go over the hill and you could run into a bunch.

Throughout the summer, the warriors took care of their hunting ponies. They even bathed them. Sometimes the horse bathed itself. They would take them to the creek wherever they were camped and let them stand in the water. While standing up, the horses would splash the water with a foreleg. They would lie down, and sometimes half roll over. They would get up, paw the water, and then lay down on the other side. But generally, a warrior who loved his pony would do this bathing for the horse. The pony understands this and stands still. The warrior would take a container and while standing beside his horse in midstream would dip the container into the water and splash water on the horse, including the tail, the mane, the underside, everywhere. The warrior took real good care of his pony.

This standing in the water and staying there for quite a while served a dual purpose. It gave the horse time to soften its hooves so they could grow out a little more. By fall, it would be like the horse was shod with horseshoes. The horse can run or turn, and even make a U-turn and not fall down, scraping the ice with that screeching sound. These ponies were surefooted.

So, the warrior took care of his pony all summer, fed him good, took him out to a good place with plenty of feed, and staked him out. They began to understand each other. The warrior would sit on top of a hill and watch him. They would talk. In doing this, the horse and rider then understood each other. They came to love each other.

The Lakota settled down for winter encampment along a river. Most generally, the camp was set up along the Missouri River. They had to select a place where there was an abundance of dry wood, a windbreak, and close to a river so they could get water. The camps were not always in the same places; they had to change year after year.

Even when they were at winter camp, stationary for the whole of winter, there came a time when the people had to have fresh meat. It could have been because of a special occasion, or because of sickness in the camp. But whatever the reason, a buffalo hunt was required in the winter. This particular hunt happened to be on a day when there was a blizzard. The warriors, being accustomed to the elements, used different ways to protect themselves. On a day such as this, they would wear a buffalo robe wrapped around their bodies, with a strip of rawhide to tie as a belt. Beneath this buffalo robe from the waist up was what you might call a deerskin shirt or jacket with fringe sleeves, back, and skirting.

For this buffalo hunt a particular warrior painted his face and his horse too. He painted the horse's legs with signs of his dreams to invoke the Great Spirit to help the horse and its rider on this special buffalo hunt. The band of warriors came upon a herd of buffalo on this day of blizzard. This warrior and his horse singled out a buffalo and chased it. Because of the blizzard, vision was sometimes next to nothing, and the singled-out buffalo turned away from the main herd. The rest of the hunters took after the main herd, but this warrior chased the lone buffalo.

For this warrior and his horse, this would not be the first kill of the day. Perhaps it was the second one. But he had to have two or three. He was thinking of those at camp who were hungry for fresh meat—the children, the elderly, the blind, the sick, the orphaned, the widowed. That is why he invoked the Great Spirit to help him get two or three buffaloes. He was on the crest of a hill, and it was very cold. Because it had probably rained before the storm, it was icy.

As the storm cleared a little, the warrior saw what looked like a stand of snakeweed at a distance. The buffalo was running toward it. Just as the warrior was about to get next to the buffalo to begin to shed his outer buffalo robe, take his bow and arrow, and put an arrow into the buffalo, some instinct told him that he must turn aside. His pony was well shod; its hooves were grown out, and the horse made a U-turn, shedding ice and making a screeching sound. His horse went skidding on the ice and turned from the edge of that huge cliff just in time and the buffalo went over. What looked to be a bunch of snakeweed were in reality the tips of huge cottonwood trees growing down at the base of the cliff. The buffalo that went over that embankment got caught halfway down in the huge crutch of one of the cottonwood trees.

It seemed to the Lakota warrior that it was a sacrifice, that no man would get to that meat. A sacrifice to the Indian is something that you offer to the Great Spirit, and to the Great Spirit alone. Because the buffalo was caught halfway up that bank, no man could get to it, although wolves, coyotes, bears, and wildcats could.

Long after the spring, the people came to that place to check on it, and what remained of the buffalo was a shrunken skeleton. And those who could come near the buffalo did not, because it was an offering to the Great Spirit, and meant for the Great Spirit alone.

This story has been told from generation to generation. It was part of what is known as the wintercount. The wintercount is drawings of events, like a calendar for each year. It is done on a stretched out, dry buffalo hide scraped clean and made pliable. The reason why they call it a wintercount is that most of the paintings on that buffalo hide are events of the winter, such as a great famine, or a great sickness that perhaps wiped out part of the tribe. Events were painted on the buffalo hide each year. They started from the center and went clockwise, coming to a full circle and starting again. This kept going until it reached the outer edges of the buffalo robe.

I remember the wintercount of the year I was born, which is 1912. In our language, that wintercount was, "When the White Cat Came to Our Camp" (Igmu Ska Wan He).

That is the story of a buffalo hunt, a warrior, and his pony—a story lovable and beautiful because the Great Spirit's hand was in it. The Great Spirit meant that buffalo to be offered to Him because this was a special, excellent warrior and his horse. The warrior could have had that buffalo. But, since it was caught in the crutch of a huge cottonwood tree, the people looked at it as an offering to the Great Spirit, and it became a wintercount event, a story to be remembered.

So, you see, man and horse functioned in unison to make life pleasant for themselves and for the people. There are songs about the wind, the streams, the mountains, the day, the night, the dawn of a new day. There are songs that pertain to the seasons of the year. And, there are songs of the horse and the buffalo too.

The Deity of the Brave

By Peter V. Catches (Zintkala Oyate)

This is a recollection of a sacred dream, as it was recounted to me. It has been necessary to carefully translate the original oral account, because of the distinct differences between the Lakota and English languages. I have under-taken this task to the best of my ability.[9]

Liquid fire splashes across the sky; the earth trembles from the roar of a thousand Thunder Beings. The circle of teepees surrounds the main fire in the center, and an opening ten lodge-lengths wide faces the east.

The landscape toward the east is a shallow meadow, with a small brook flowing through the high underbrush. The hills above the brook are covered with a blanket of pine, natural to this environment. In the meadow is the herd of stallions that belongs to the Lakota oyate encampment.

West of the encampment lies the prairie, with its sea of natural grass as high as a man's waist. Closer to the encampment is a lone hill, a lone breast coming out of Mother Earth. There a shadowed figure is seen walking, walking slowly in a manner none can understand.

Around the main fire inside the encampment stand the dog warriors, who were the night guard. They have come in, having been replaced by the day guard. Some of the people of the village are now beginning to move about. It is dawn.

Flashes of light blind those who look up. A shaking of the earth and a crashing noise wake those who still sleep. The stallions in the meadow are restlessly milling about, as if wondering if some unseen fury may be about to descend upon them. The shadowy figure slowly continues to walk up the lone hill. He is unmindful of the eyes that still watch him from the camp. The voices of the people are muffled, their hands are pointed, and their unswerving attention is attracted to this lone figure as he slowly continues to walk in a way none had ever seen before.

In the meadow, the air is thick and still, and then there is a flash of lightning with a thunderclap of a kind that one will hear once in a lifetime. The earth quakes enough to chill the blood. The consciousness of the people in the camp, Lakota oyate, knows this pattern, for they have seen and felt such things at other times. They know that the loving hand of the Great Spirit is about to touch one of His children.

From the meadow, there comes a loud neighing, and from among the milling herd, a horse like no other darts forth. Huge in stature, it is as if three horses had become one, yet this horse controls its rhythm as only a deer would. It jumps, darts, and kicks in the air as if crazed.

The figure can now be seen at the very top of the hill, with his arms outstretched toward the heavens. Lightning seems to be touching his hands with every flash and resounding, echoing clap of thunder. The horse seems responsible for the shaking of the earth, as it gallops wildly toward the lone figure still standing with his arms outstretched toward the heavens.

The dog warriors and the awakened people watch in wonder and amazement. It seems as though everything is now occurring in slow motion. Big drops of rain can be distinctly seen as they slowly fall. Each person's next heartbeat seems to be an eternity away. All can feel themselves breathing each molecule of air, one at a time.

The maddened horse has turned, and suddenly reaches the camp. Everyone is alarmed, and yet nothing is done, for nothing can be done. Now the oyate see that this horse is foaming at the mouth. The horse has been dancing, bucking, jumping, and rearing up. Again it turns toward the hill, the lone hill toward the west, and rears up for the last time. It takes off at a full gallop in the direction of the hill, where the lone figure still stands with hands outstretched toward the heavens.

The main medicine man in the encampment of the Lakota oyate gathers about him the sacred drum singers, for they know the songs of the people, the first people of peace. They know the songs of birth, of living life, and of death itself. He moves slowly, deliberately, with the full wisdom befitting one chosen to be above other holy men. His station was ordained by destiny, just as was the Mother, our Earth, destined to travel around the sun. Some portions of one's life are simply part of a greater purpose.

The medicine man is old; life has stamped the creases of myriad lines upon his face. They have been beautifully carved, moment by moment, by the fingers of time's emotions, and behind this inscription is the wisdom of the ages handed down from generation to generation in experiential teachings. He too had visions. He too had psychic dreams. He too had inclinations. And he had possessed, in all of his years, the ability to relive such moments again and again. He knew very well of this perfection; it had become a symbiotic part of him. The Great Mystery had revealed these moments to him, and now he is prepared. He will do his part and do it well.

The frenzied horse is a dappled gray, a magnificent creature. Lucidly flowing, it slowly rushes in a dreamlike gallop. Its color is a faint sky blue in the awakening dawn. The holy man had seen this reality before, and now how frighteningly wonderful it is to be a part of this mystery. He remembers the before and the after; and now, he hears the living, the crying—the crying he had heard many times.

In the quiet of the meadow, in the stillness of the cool crisp air, a dear and resounding voice can be heard. It is a voice in the beginning of this chant:

> *Tunkasila wa mung yanka yo*
> *Le miyaca nawajin yelo*

>>>→ • ←<<<

Wa mung yanka yo
Le miyaca nawajin yelo

Tunkasila wa mung yanka yo
Le miyaca nawajin yelo
Wa mung yanka yo
Le miyaca nawajin yelo

Grandfathers, look at me
This is I who is standing
Look at me
This is I who is standing

The echoing chant reverberates in the meadow, which is quiet no longer. The sacred drum singers beat the drum in rhythmic unison, and the sound of the gushing chant becomes a song of vision.

The shadowed lone figure is no longer alone. The horse and the man have become absorbed in one; they have become one spirit. This man, this warrior, is personified, and has become a link between the material physical world and the beyond of the spiritual world.

That old wrinkled medicine man of so many years had already known that this part of the vision was to be a reality. And he is quiet as he sits now in the dark serene silence of the Inipi. He hears the guttural voices no longer. The visions are gone, and there to his right at the back of the lodge sits the warrior. He knows what this warrior must do in the years to come. It will be his destiny to live the visions, and to make them into reality upon this earth. He knows that this warrior is special, that he is the epitome of the brave, the Deity of the Brave.

The Legend of Pte Woku

By Peter V. Catches (Zintkala Oyate)

This is how the legend was told to me by Petaga Yuha Mani. He in turn was told the legend by Alfred Ribsman, a survivor of the Wounded Knee Massacre, who was my maternal grandfather.

The valley where we have the annual Pte Woku (Feeding of the Buffalo) Sundance was once known as Red Feather Valley. Pte Woku valley is now a part of the Calico community and is known as a very special place. The valley is a place of such spiritual presence that many people go there to do their fasts. My father did his first and most personal Sundance there in the summer of 1964, and for the past fourteen years, I have conducted the Sundance in this valley. One of the stories which took place in the Pte Woku valley is about a young man in his late twenties or early thirties who had done a Hanbleceya in a certain area near a high butte, which can be seen from a few miles away. It is generally called Mission Butte, because the Catholic mission school was nearby.

This young man's fast took place in the early 1920s. The exact location of his Hanbleceya was right on top of the butte. He was to fast for four days and four nights, but on the second morning when the medicine man watching over him went there to check up on him, the young man was gone. There were no tracks on the soft earth, no disturbances of any kind indicating that he had left the area where he had been designated to pray to the Great Mystery.

Those were the horse-and-buggy days, and there were no means of fast communication. So, his family sent out runners on horseback to nearby towns, and even to other states and other tribes, to see if anyone of that description had been seen passing through the area. No one had even so much as heard of him, let alone seen him. The story goes that, being a good soul, he had simply gone from that hilltop right into the Land of the Winds.

Another legend about this place occurred in the 1830s. The Lakota oyate were camped nearby in the springtime of the year. Because it was spring, the food supply was low, and the people were hungry. Warriors were sent out from the encampment to see if they could capture some small game, since there were no buffalo herds close by. Scout warriors were sent out in every direction.

When one warrior came upon the Red Feather Valley, he decided to explore the entire area. As midday approached, he climbed a hill with a long ridge covered with pines. Once on top, he sat down on the ground in the shade of one of the large conifers that overlooked the valley. Since it was midday, he decided to have his meal of *papa* (dried meat) and drink some water from his bladder container.

The long ridged hill where he rested stands north of our Sundance grounds of today. As he sat there resting and eating in the coolness of the shade, he gazed about and noticed the beauty of the place. Then he noticed something different, something out of place, on the other side of the valley. From where the warrior sat, he had a clear view down a steep incline to a creek bottom. The creek is fed by natural springs farther up the valley. On the other side of the creek bottom, which is thick with ash, elm, and other trees and shrubs indigenous to the area, there is another steep sloping hill, which rises up to a large flat area. This flat area is where the warrior had seen something unusual. Something had stirred inside of him. He felt strange emotions, unlike the natural highs and lows one might feel on any ordinary day.

He felt a deep apprehension, and he needed to know what had stirred those feelings inside. He arose, went down the ridge, and crossed the creek. He deliberately and slowly made his way up the hill leading to the flat area. As he cautiously peered over onto the flat area, he noticed that at its back, near the tree line, and somewhat to the east, there was a buffalo lying down. His first thought was to retrieve an arrow and thread it to his bowstring, which he did.

But as he continued to watch, he came to the conclusion that the buffalo was already dead. He put the arrow back into his quiver, shouldered his bow, and slowly approached the huge bison. By the looks of it, he thought it had to be a three-year-old bull. But he was not sure and needed to take a closer look.

As he approached the bison bull, he noticed that it was breathing, but that its breaths were very shallow. He moved closer still and put his ear to its neck by its throat. He could hear the faintest slow beat of its heart. His next thoughts were confused. "Why is this lone buffalo here? Why is he not near the cool streams where there is shade and the tender sprouts of new grass? Did the Great Mystery put this bull here for me to kill and take back to the people? Why is it that I feel that it is meant to live, and that I am to nurse it back to life?"

Being a Lakota, he understood that the bison and his nation were brothers, and he decided to go with the last thought. He felt reinforced by the extraordinary nature of this situation. He was uplifted by his affirmation, and was sure that the Great Mystery approved of his decision.

With that he went down to the stream and filled up his bladder container. He cut two heaping armfuls of the fresh grass and went back up to where the buffalo lay. With deliberate earnestness, he petted and talked to his brother. "Take this food, and eat it. It is medicine. Take this water, and drink it. It is medicine." As their eyes met an understanding was made, and the buffalo ate some grass and drank some water, even though as the warrior noticed, it took just a little. Nevertheless, he knew through experience that the healing had started.

He stayed there for a time, and in the evening he started back to his camp, but not before telling his brother that he would take care of him until he got well, and not to be afraid, for he would be watching over him. With that, he started back to his camp.

On the way back to camp, he felt that he had done the right thing about that day's happening. At the same time, he felt empty, because he was sent out to find food, and he was bringing nothing back. He had nothing to show for his day's hunt. As the warrior approached the encampment of his people, he heard drums. He heard the shouts and yells of happiness. His spirit soared as he entered the circle of the village and discovered that all of the other warriors had been very successful, and that a big celebration was underway.

The people were happy and milled around a huge bonfire as each warrior took a turn relating what he had encountered in that day. The people listened with enthusiastic imaginations and yelled whoops of approval and agreement, verifying that they would have done the same as the warriors had they been in their place.

Now it came to the turn of the warrior who had gone to the Red Feather Valley to talk about his day and tell what had happened during his hunt. The scout warrior stood up, and the people, realizing that this was the one warrior who had come back empty-handed, listened with great curiosity to his story.

After he had completed his tale, he described the location where the bison bull laid. He asked if he had made a right decision. There was a great deal of conversation then, and finally one of the spiritual elders stood up and said, "Human emotion cannot be denied. Spiritual matters are a factor in the development of understanding. Reason is a part of the creative force of all things in the Holy Swirl of the universe. Why is that buffalo there, alone and separated from his herd, sick, hungry, and dying? It is this warrior's honor of obligation to do the things he said to the buffalo, and later on, if the Great Mystery, the All Knowing, shows us why this is so, then that too is good! The entire camp will stay at this spot until there is a change."

With all approving, the elder silently sat down. Then the warrior stood up and told everyone to stay away from that particular area. The celebration continued until dawn.

For the next week and into the following week, the warrior fed and brought cool water to drink to his brother. Then one morning, while he watched, the bison began to struggle. First he got onto his knees, and then onto one leg. Then he fought his way up to two legs, and finally he was standing. The warrior's bison brother was still very weak and staggered about as he walked, and yet the warrior felt that rush of joy, sensed the continuation of the miracle of life, under even these bleak circumstances. He was very happy, and tears welled up in his eyes as he saw the look and expression of acknowledgment in his brother's gaze.

The warrior began to look forward to spending time with his brother every morning. He noticed that with each passing day the bison got stronger and pawed more and more at the earth with his hooves, and dug even more energetically at it with his horns. In the evenings, you could hear the bellowing of his bison brother for miles.

One morning the scout warrior found that his spirit brother was gone. His immediate reaction was of panic and alarm. He searched the entire area to no avail. He knew now that his spirit brother had gone back to his own people and he felt very sad at this loss. He took his sadness back to the encampment with him. He took it to the medicine man, and with a heavy heart told of the things he felt, of the bond that was made between him and his spirit brother. The medicine man sat in silence for a while, and then he said, "That bond will always be there in its time where it belongs. You must cherish those moments, and in some way, they will help you to understand and to continue on."

The whole camp prepared to move to another location when they heard that the buffalo had gotten well. In that particular band of the nation, it is said that the year was known as the year when the buffalo got well. Many years passed, perhaps eighteen or nineteen, when this particular band found itself isolated in the Badlands, in what is now South Dakota. They were caught in a huge snowstorm, a real blizzard. Their food supply was nearly gone, and so they sent out scout warriors to hunt, but the buffalo's brother was not included among them. He was now old and weak, and it was feared that he might die in the icy cold of the blinding storm.

But the buffalo's brother was not pleased to be left behind. He went to the village's *naca* (leader) and pleaded with him. He explained that all of his life he had toiled for the benefit of others. He stated that he was a servant of the people. He declared that within his heart—a warrior's heart—he knew that if he should die in the storm, striving to protect the people, he would die willingly, as was the way of his spirit. The naca let him go.

Back in his lodge, he spoke solemnly to his wife. "Be strong, and if I don't come back, do not worry, we will see each other again." With that, he left. As he left the sheltered windbreak of the teepees, he could only see a few feet in front of his face. There was blinding whiteness everywhere he looked, and so he decided to go with the wind, for that would save his energy. That night he slept in a crevice.

In the morning he got up and jumped around to circulate his blood. The storm was raging like the day before, and he continued until he ran right into something. It had fur and was warm, and the old warrior was excited, but he was also weak from the icy cold that engulfed him. To his surprise, the bull laid down with his back to the wind. So the old warrior laid right down next to him, up against the belly of that old bull, and became warm.

After a time, the old bull started to move and get up onto his feet. Upon standing, it seemed as if he was waiting for something. So the old warrior got up and started to feel the old bull. That power or essence known to us as *nagi* (spirit) flowed gently, and there was recognition as the bull bellowed several times. At that moment, the old warrior really knew. The bull now was also old, and yet he was huge. He started to walk slowly away from the old warrior and stopped as if to wait. The warrior knew then what to do, and he grabbed hold of the bull's tail and followed behind him until it grew dark. Then the old buffalo laid down as before, and the old warrior warmed up again, laying against the belly of his spirit brother.

When they started up again the next day, the blizzard was worse than before. They traveled slowly until the old bull finally stopped and laid down. The old warrior scout began to really understand what was going on when he realized that he was back at the encampment of his people. He yelled out a loud *akisa* (war whoop), and the people came

Petaga Yuha Mani in traditional home (teepee) with
altar in foreground.

running to where he stood. When he turned around to look at his brother who still laid there, he saw that the spark of life was gone. In this legend, we find that the warrior and the bison bull had come full circle in each other in order to fulfill a greater purpose in life.

Truth and Honesty

In my early life I went to a Jesuit school, where one of the concepts that makes up the religion is to never lie. The missionary who taught religious instruction in a catechism class stressed the fact that truth and honesty are the best means of living a good life. He emphasized his instructions by telling stories.

The missionary said we must be very careful of how we live in this world—even to the point of what one red penny could do. One red penny is nearly worthless by itself, but ninety-nine others make one dollar. If someone kept a penny meant for the people, that would hinder the person's entry into heaven. So, he stressed the fact that honesty is the most vital part for anyone serving the public.

I often recall those stories I heard as a young man; they meant so much to me. Although I do not follow the Jesuit religion anymore, I know that some of the values we were taught are good. One of the things I want to make clear is that I do not claim to know it all. As human beings, we all make mistakes. I think it was these stories that kept me from going too much into the bad way of life. As a human being, I too have my faults. I am impatient at times, and I get angry at times. It is like this with the tribal government and the many areas and departments that serve the people. The people who serve in those departments are human beings, and they like to play favorites, and they like to be underhanded sometimes. I do not claim that I am not that way; I try hard not to be. I am saying that I am not the judge. I am not saying that all the rest of the world is no good. There are good people in the world; there is good in all peoples.

Honesty is one of the essential things. It is very, very important that we be honest, not only with others, but most especially with ourselves. We must be honest with ourselves, and that way, if it comes from within us, then we know we can be honest with everyone around us that we come in contact with.

Honesty to me is so great a value that all people should make it a custom as long as we are in this world. It is one of the foundations that could bring about peace. Even a powerful nation like the United States is sometimes lacking in honesty. The U.S. government, if it were honest, would uphold the treaties that it made with Native Americans.

I will tell you a tale about honesty. I will not mention names, because this man is related to us and people living now know him. In the fall of the year, in the covered-wagon days, this young warrior was part of an encampment of Indian people. The warriors, known as dog soldiers and as the Tokala (Kit Fox) society, did a lot of work in the camp. They kept the main fire going throughout the day and the night so that if one of the smaller fires elsewhere in the camp went out, the people would take from the main fire and start their fires again. The Tokala society also took care of the elderly and the sick. After a hunt, they brought back buffalo meat to those in need—the orphans, old, weak, sick, and widowed.

Throughout our history, kept in oral traditions, the Indian people have taken care of their own needs, because this was the way of life fashioned by the Great Spirit and infused in the hearts and minds of the Indian people. Our name, Lakota, means "Peace." We are a peaceful people. Only when our hunting territory was invaded did we act to protect ourselves.

But like anywhere else and in any organization, there is bound to be some group that tries to bring disharmony. One fall night, some young men in the camp got together and sneaked off to waylay a covered-wagon train. In a fight such as this, they might take the oxen or horses that drew the wagons in order to stop the wagon train and then let people go, or they might choose to handle the situation differently according to their plan of warfare. On this night, the young men stopped a wagon and killed the men, women, and everyone else who was part of the wagon train. The only exception was one young girl. They set fire to everything, killed the teams of horses, and took captive the one white girl.

At the time the policy of Indian encampments was that when someone was taken prisoner, the matter would have to be taken before the "council fire." They would have a council in the evening with a bonfire burning. At the council fire, people with any attachment to the issue at hand were given time to talk.

So, the white girl was taken before the council fire. Those who captured her and brought her back explained the situation. This honest warrior was sitting there listening to what was being said. In the ensuing talk about what to do with the white girl, the honest warrior stood up and told the council that he was married to a good woman and his intentions were not upon another woman. He stated that what he had was what he wanted, and he did not want anything more. He then told the white girl's story in such a way that people listened real closely.

"This white girl's parents, uncles or aunts, or whomever, have been wiped away, so this white girl is grieving. She is in sorrow. I want this white girl to live in my home, and my wife will take care of her. We will give her the choicest of meat to eat, give her a place of honor with many buffalo hides to sleep on, and keep her warm through the winter months. In the spring, when the ponies are fed and grow fat and lively, when new life is born in the ponies, I will select two honest warriors to go with me to take this white girl to the nearest army post."

The chiefs in charge of this council fire decided that this was the best they had heard, and they gave this honest warrior the white girl to care for. He took her back to his camp and explained to his wife that she was in charge of her and that she was to feed her first because she was an honored guest. The wife was to give her the best of the meat, and when she drew fresh water, to give her the first drink. Lastly, the wife was to go with the girl to the bathroom, or wherever she went, and watch over her so she would not be afraid.

Because of the warrior's intent and preparations, the white girl was well taken care of through the winter months. Her grieving for her lost relatives soon faded away—time heals all pain and time heals all sorrow. She was taught to learn the sign language. In midwinter, she could be heard to laugh, and she began to understand the language that we speak.

The winter months quickly passed and spring came upon the Indian encampment. Ice melted in the streams. Greening began to show itself—green grass and buds on the trees. Ponies were cropping the green grass and began to grow fat. As was the custom of the time, scouts were sent out. The honest warrior told the scouts to discover the location of the closest army post. They scouted the countryside and along a big river, and soon came upon a fort. Distances were gauged by travel during a day, and the scouts estimated that it was a three-day ride to the army post.

When the virtuous warrior was informed of the distance by the scouts, he selected two honest warriors to go with him to take the white girl to the army post. They traveled slowly, and on the third day, they arrived at the army post. At that time it was customary that, when you were on horseback, you would turn sideways on the horizon for the people at the post to see you. You would then turn the other way and show your flag of truce, an indication that the two sides could talk, or parley. If the people in the fort accepted the parley, they would signal by opening the big gates. So, when the three warriors arrived at the horizon overlooking the fort, they showed themselves by turning the horses sideways. Through their field glasses, the soldiers at the fort saw three Indian warriors and one white girl, and so they threw open the fort gates. The warriors walked their horses slowly. When they entered the fort, the infantry was all lined up with the cavalry behind them, and the army commanders were standing near the flagpole.

The Indians rode to the center. The white girl jumped off her horse, ran to the captain, pointed to the honest warriors, and said, "They raped me. I was captured in the fall and they treated me mean all through the winter." So, instead of respect for the good thing that they did, for the good deed they had done, the Indians were imprisoned. They were put in irons and thrown into a cell. The army post commanders had a meeting to see what they should do with the three warriors. After days of searching for a solution, they finally agreed to kill them. The general went to see the prisoners and told them, "When the sun comes up, we will take you three on horseback out that way. There is a hill, a long hill. We will go up on that hill and go to the very end to a point over there and shoot you." He said this, but he used motions so that the Indians would understand. The honest warrior agreed to what was being communicated.

Throughout the time that the Indians were imprisoned, a ball and chain was fastened to their ankles. The same chain was fastened around their wrists. It was awkward, and made of heavy iron so it cut into their flesh. The least movement they made was painful and irritating.

The next morning the soldiers fed them good, and the warriors were readied and mounted. Through the night, the honest warrior was telling the others, "I will give one word, *hokahey*." Every Indian, even today, knows what that word means, "go full speed ahead to your right."

Only one horse had a lead rope to a soldier. The rest were tied together. From the first horse and rider, the lead rope was tied to the second, and from the second horse, the lead rope was tied to the third rider's horse. The Indians and soldiers rode to the hill and knew when they had arrived. The Indians talked to one another with their eyes. When they were coming to the point to where they were going to be shot, the honest warrior turned his head. That little movement told the others to be ready. He hollered, "hokahey!" And the horses as one went forward so quickly and so powerfully that the lead rope held by the soldier came away. The warriors and their horses went down that hill running all out. The soldiers were so taken by surprise that they could not get their pistols out, and by the time the soldiers could take aim the warriors were out of range.

There were big bushes and sagebrush everywhere—it must have been in Wyoming country. The warriors had to jump or go around the brush, but they were all running smoothly; none of them tripped, although they were still tied together. The Indian ponies at that time were used to buffalo hunts and running like that. You had to use your knees to guide the horses and they would instantly obey. It is said that at that time, the Indian rider and his horse were like one machine working in harmony to perfection. There was no need for a whip. Just a holler of "hokahey," and the horse would give all that he had.

The previous night there must have been a downpour in that region, because the Indians came upon a swollen river and stopped at the bank. The honest warrior held up his hands and said, "Great Spirit, help us through this stream. If you help us escape, I will dance the Sundance next summer."

The honest warrior said next summer, not this summer. Today we would most likely say "this summer." But traditionally, a ceremony such as the Sundance or the Pipefast required one solid year of preparation. They had to prepare to have their Pipe in order, and the essential parts to make up their regalia. And most of all, they had to internally prepare themselves, such as avoiding anger and trying to be honest, because when they approach that sacred place, they will go in the presence of the Great Spirit. If they have impure things inside of themselves, such as dishonesty, unkindness, being quarrelsome, and other such things, the Great Spirit will not be at that sacred place.

So the honest warrior raised his hand and said, "Great Spirit, help me. Help us through this stream. Help us escape and I will dance the Sundance next year, next summer." Summer was just two or three months away, but he meant the next summer, for he needed preparation time to be ready.

They say that the warriors and their ponies trotted through the flood, and the water went just above the knees of the horses that they rode. Seeing what happened when the

Indians crossed, the pursuing soldiers rushed ahead into the stream. It was deep, so when they rushed in there, they fell into the deep water. One horse was drowned and its rider nearly drowned too. How did it happen that the stream was shallow, just above the knees of the horses, when these three Indians passed through the stream, but when the soldiers came, it was a deep raging flood where a horse drowned?

The story goes on to say that, after their escape, the honest warrior prepared himself from that summer through the ensuing months, through the following winter, and on into the next summer. By the time the next summer came, he was ready. He pierced both sides of his chest the first day, and he danced, fighting the rawhide thongs that were tied to the Sundance Tree for four days, sometimes falling from sheer exhaustion. But he fulfilled his promise to the Great Spirit that, if they escaped from the pursuing soldiers, he would dance the Sundance.

The warrior fulfilled his promise, and he related his story in the years after. His wrists and ankles were scarred from the ball and chains for the rest of his life, in testimony of an honest warrior who would go far to do a good deed for one of his fellow human beings. Before he passed from this world, he said, "My wrists and my ankles bear the scars of honesty. You can be scarred by being honest, but the Great Spirit loves you all the more because of your honesty."

Wounded Knee, 1973

On December 29, 1890, U.S. Cavalry soldiers attacked the encampment of Chief Big Foot of the Oglala Lakota

»»—→ • ←—«««

near Wounded Knee Creek. Between 300 and 500 Lakota were killed that day.[10] On February 28, 1973, American Indian Movement (AIM) activists and local Oglala Lakota seized the village of Wounded Knee on the Pine Ridge Reservation in South Dakota for seventy-one days. Their purpose was to use the seizure of the site— which for many Lakota continues to be a wound in their collective memory—as a temporary platform from which to publicize grievances.[11]

I was in the hospital undergoing major surgery in January 1973 at Ellsworth Air Force Base Hospital. In that surgery, forty percent of my stomach was removed. I nearly left this world at that time. I have said why I think the Great Spirit does things so mysteriously; that when people think they can leave this world, they are kept living here. In my life, I have experienced many occasions when I could have died.

When I went through this major surgery in January 1973, I had a difficult time getting back. I was in intensive care for a long time. The time that I spent in intensive care is a story in itself, because I was near death. You might say I was near the doorway of entering into the Great Hereafter, but I lingered there. Drugs were inserted into me so that I would not feel the pain.

Oftentimes, maybe because of the drugs that were given to me, I would fade away not knowing anything. But looking back on that time, I can picture it very clearly. One night I awakened, and it was pretty hard to clear the cobwebs in my brain. I was hearing a certain amount of drumming, like mumbling. When my mind cleared, I saw an old nurse, one of those who was taking care of me in intensive care. She was kneeling by my bedside around about the area of my knees, and she was reciting the rosary, the Catholic prayer. I was listening to it; I got caught up with the prayer.

I thought, "How is it that a nurse, doing all she can do, taking care of a near-dying patient, can set out her heart over and beyond what she is expected to do and spend some time kneeling by the bedside of a patient and pray the rosary?" That to me is doing something beyond the call of duty, beyond what she is supposed to do. It is true devotion, a true mark of her profession in trying to help a patient. She understood that the medical world in this physical world of ours was slow in making me well, and she was imploring the supernatural, the Virgin Mary, and praying the rosary to assist me in my recovery. That to me is excellence, a shining example of the profession of a nurse tending to a patient.

When I was recovering, I developed pneumonia. To make matters worse, when the bandages were removed, I wanted to scratch the wound. This was an indication that it was getting well, but then I noticed pus in between the stitches, and I pointed this out to the male nurses who tended to me. They called the doctor and he cut open the stitches. This open wound infection had to be scraped off every other day and irrigated. They had to cleanse it with some medicine to help heal the infection.

I was released back to the Pine Ridge Reservation Indian Health Service Hospital, and I spent several weeks there in February. Because of a shortage of beds, on February

24 I volunteered to go home. I was off intravenous feeding for over a week and able to walk around, so I thought I could manage going home. But the doctor said I was to come in every other day to have my surgery wound tended to.

When I was home a couple of days, there was a meeting occurring at Calico Hall in the small community called Calico, a little over four miles north of Pine Ridge on U.S. Highway 18, going toward Hot Springs. People came to this meeting from all over the reservation. Every district had a sort of headquarters, such as Oglala, Porcupine, Kyle, Manderson, Wamble, Allen, those places. Every district was represented there, even church people. The reason behind this meeting was Richard Wilson, chairman of the Oglala Sioux Tribal Council. He was, with the help of the Bureau of Indian Affairs (BIA) and the U.S. government, acting like a dictator. He had his so-called "goons" travel the highways and the districts. These goons were keeping tabs on the people who did not like what Dick Wilson was doing.

People could not get together to communicate. We could not hold meetings. No three people could get together and talk. Even when they talked about the weather, people in groups were broken up by Dick Wilson's goons. These goons were everywhere. Dick Wilson saw to it that everything the goons needed was provided for, such as the fuel for their cars, and the whiskey that they enjoyed drinking to give them false courage. They would go around shooting off their rifles and shooting off their mouths.

The voting precincts had been corrupted. Everyone on the reservation knew this. At the voting precincts, people who voted for Dick Wilson were paid in kind with a pint of wine. This was observed by the people at large. When a person got drunk and thrown in jail, he was abused, knocked around, that sort of thing. Nothing went right. There was a real power struggle. The people knowing these things got together at Calico and talked about the situation. In trying to put an end to it, they called in the American Indian Movement to sit in on one of these meetings and try to arrive at a solution. I believe this was the night of February 26. We had a secret meeting and people were chosen at random to go to the Advent Church, which was just a few hundred yards from the Calico meeting hall. In the basement of the church, there was quite a gathering of the people chosen to represent the districts that made up the reservation.

One of the chosen people selected to be at that meeting was myself, even as sick as I was. I could hardly sit up for twenty or twenty-five minutes at a time. I was tired, still weak, and had lost a lot of weight. All I wanted to do was lie in bed. I did not even care to eat, because it was stomach surgery and a lot of the foods I was supposed to eat did not agree with me. The recommended foods were milk and a bland sort of soup. I could not eat fried food. Things I could eat, like potatoes, had to be steam cooked, and I could not eat very much. So, I was ill at ease and my disposition was not up to par.

Anyway, at that very secret meeting the district representatives arrived at a solution. They decided to organize a car caravan and take over Wounded Knee. Bits of the talk touched on Wounded Knee 1890, how the government and the 7th Cavalry committed a most shameful act in disposing of the weapons of the Indians, encircling them, and then firing upon them. I believe this was the most shameful act of the U.S. government. People talk about the Mylai massacre in Vietnam, a shameful act. Mylai happened that way, yes, but the start of Mylai in Vietnam was Wounded Knee on the Pine Ridge Indian Reservation in 1890. So, history repeats itself. The soldiers of the 7th Cavalry were honored. They were even given Congressional Medals of Honor for this cruel act of genocide.

According to our customs, we believe we live in a world where the spirits of our relatives who have gone before us are still very close to us. This is how Wakan Tanka made us a special people. We do not ever forget our dead, most especially those that were slaughtered in the way the people were slaughtered at Wounded Knee in 1890. So, we figured that if we in 1973 would go into Wounded Knee and take over Wounded Knee, the spirits of the dead of 1890 would help us. We are closely related. This is what relationship means to Indian people.

We went back to the meeting hall in Calico, and the leader told the people what we intended to do. He said we are going into Wounded Knee and anybody wishing to come along may do so. He said it in a way that was understood by people who did not like the system we were in. With the backing of the BIA and the U.S. government, Dick Wilson and the tribal council were overruling the people. This was a wrong plainly seen by everybody. We were pushed aside, treated as if we were nothing. We were not a people to them. That was the feeling we had.

So, the people got together and they started their cars. But like I said, I could not stay in a sitting position for more than twenty or twenty-five minutes, and I was tired after the meeting at Calico Hall and the one in the basement of the church. I was overly tired and I wanted to lie down. My family and I stayed behind. When all the cars had taken off, we went along as far as our branch-off at Mission Flat, and then we turned to home.

When we got home, the house was cold. We built a fire and I went straight to bed. When it was warm, I got up, stood by the stove, and warmed myself. I missed the hospital because in the hospital I did not feel the chill or any unpleasantness. When I wanted medicine they gave it to me, and the room was always at average warmth. At home, we have to build a fire. Sometimes the fire is too hot, sometimes not as hot. When we go to bed at night, about an hour and a half after we all retire to sleep, the fire goes out. In the morning, it is cold like an icehouse. Someone has to get up and start a fire.

I stood there warming myself and thinking, "Why did I ever come away from the hospital, being sickly and very weak, when I could have been resting there? And in the condition I am in, why did I become involved in the cares and problems that confront the tribe? How did I become a part of the meetings and the selected group that met at the church basement?" I realized that being an Indian is the hardest thing to be in this age, as long as the dominant society has control over everything. We have to have permits for everything. And when you want to go after something, the red tape that you have to go through is so discouraging.

The next day after breakfast I wanted to go to town. I wanted to go to the courthouse and do some business there. When I entered the courthouse, a policeman told me someone wanted to see me in the BIA superintendent's office right away. We got in his car and went to the superintendent's office. When I entered his office, there was a lone Indian sitting there, my *tahansi* (cousin), Frank Fools Crow. We shook hands. I sat down and he said, "I do not know what they are up to, but they told me to come here, and here I am." So, I told him, "It is the same thing with me. They told me they wanted to see me here and so I, too, came to see what was the matter."

When the superintendent came in, he told Frank and me, "The condition that we are facing now is that a car caravan has taken over Wounded Knee, and roadblocks were set up so no one can come out or get into Wounded Knee. Six people have been selected to go into Wounded Knee and see the conditions there, talk to the people there, and try to negotiate a quiet settlement, so no one will get hurt and no one will get killed."

The superintendent mentioned the names of the people who were selected: Charlie Red Cloud, Edgar Red Cloud, Frank Fools Crow, Seivert Young Bear, Tom Bad Cob, and myself. These six were selected reservation-wide because we understood the part of the reservation that we lived in. And since it was a reservation-wide movement that went into Wounded Knee, we all had to talk to our people, try to negotiate with the BIA, the goon squad, and Dick Wilson's outfit.

By that time, I think the U.S. Marshals were present. I am not sure of that, but they did not waste time getting there. They wanted Frank and me to go to Wounded Knee right away. They said the other four would eventually get there. A car with a driver was provided that would take us to what they called a DMZ (demilitarized zone).

Roadblocks had been set up by the people. The roadblocks there were really efficient. There are four entrances or arteries leading into Wounded Knee. The highway from Pine Ridge and the road from Manderson come to Wounded Knee. The road from Porcupine and the road from the Denby area and Gordon, Nebraska area come through Wounded Knee. So, there are four arteries of travel, and all of these roads were blocked. The cars that went through had to stop and be inspected. People who were not trying to help were turned back.

We came to the point called the DMZ; the AIM guards stopped the car. Oscar Bear Runner was in charge of the route that goes into Wounded Knee. They came over and inspected us. They recognized us, and we shook hands and explained why we came. They let us through. Frank and I had to get out of the car at that point and walk into Wounded Knee, which was quite a ways, about a mile.

There were live M–16 bullets pouring into Wounded Knee at the time I went in there. Soon after arriving in Wounded Knee, we had a meeting with those who were there. We talked about the purpose of our visit. Frank asked me to talk first. I told them I was glad to see them, that I knew most of them, and being Lakota, we understand each other. I said the reason I came was that the superintendent, those in charge, perhaps the Marshals, perhaps the FBI, were eager to negotiate with those people in Wounded Knee to set their arms aside and come to terms. They wanted us to seek negotiations to avoid further harm.

I said, "Deep down in my heart, I am with you people. I was with you people during the meetings at Calico Hall, and the meeting held in the basement of the church close by Calico Hall. I was in this all the way through. My heart is involved, even though I am a sick man, even though I should be at home and be recuperating from this present state of my health."

Many people did not know I went through a major operation. I explained, "I am still weak and cannot eat very much, or very many foods. Even the foods that I can eat by doctor's orders I cannot eat. I live in this sort of misery. But then came the call of the need to be with the Lakota people, and this call was strong in my heart. I had to come because I was called upon to do something that would lead to shaking hands all around, to come to an understanding, and to present to the BIA, the Marshals, and the U.S. government, that Dick Wilson is the cause of this taking over of Wounded Knee."

A person living like Dick Wilson did is not Lakota. One of the traditions of the Lakota heritage is that any Indian firing upon another Indian, especially with intent to kill or to do bodily harm, is not Lakota. All my life this has been my belief, and all those who died in 1890 have the same feeling. The people of the Lakota Nation, all who are traditional, will say the same words I am saying now. Those so-called Lakotas, who fired into Wounded Knee at that time in 1973, are not Lakota. They should go to a white community and see if they can do that over there. So, I say that what happened in Wounded Knee in 1973 will never ever be forgiven.

I stayed in Wounded Knee for seven days. Frank Fools Crow and the others left after the first meeting but came back almost every day. Day and night you could hear incoming M–16s and machine guns out there, rat-a-tat-tat-tat, like that. When people in the area walked in plain sight, the machine guns from the FBI roadblocks up on the hill toward Denby fired into Wounded Knee, close by where people were walking, just to harass them. The shots were fired by some ranchers living there, and of course, by the Marshals and the FBI. I know they purposely did not hit anyone, but they wanted people in Wounded Knee to know they were using live bullets. They used these scare tactics to try and make the people submit to the outcome that the dominant society wished for at Wounded Knee.

I want to mention that Charlie and Edgar Red Cloud did not go into Wounded Knee. The other three—Tom Bad Cobb, Seivert Young Bear, and Frank Fools Crow—made daily trips into Wounded Knee. I remember Frank on his arrival. He had his tobacco bag. In that tobacco bag were Bull Durham, cigarettes, and medicine, because he is a medicine man. He carried these inside for the people in Wounded Knee.

The FBI and the Marshals set up their own heavily guarded roadblocks. Every night flares were sent in the direction of the Indian encampment. The local Indians knew the avenues of escape from Wounded Knee and would sneak out during the night. When they reached home, they would talk to people about conditions at Wounded Knee. They would pack up food supplies and camp goods, such as beans, rice, cornmeal, flour, baking powder, tobacco, aspirins, cold pills, and so forth. They would rest for a while, get these supplies together, put them in a knapsack, and carry them back to Wounded Knee through the night.

All the time that the siege was held by the FBI, Marshals, and Dick Wilson's goons, the traffic coming in and out of Wounded Knee at night was wide open. There are some good stories about Wounded Knee at that time. Even birds and owls helped Lakota people to find their way into or out of Wounded Knee. A lot of people gathered in the church basement at Wounded Knee to be out of the cold.

It is almost always cold in the month of February on the Pine Ridge Indian Reservation. It seemed to me that the doorway was never shut for a minute day or night with the constant goings and comings. I was in that basement, and I noticed that everybody had the sniffles or some sort of cold. There was coughing there, and we did not have medicine.

The doctor at the Indian Health Service Hospital was Dr. Nodebaum. He was a very good doctor, very close, dedicated, and devoted to the people he served. They told me that he searched for me the first day that I did not show up at Pine Ridge Hospital to have my wound cleansed and irrigated, and to change bandages. He was worried about me.

I was taking a terrible risk. I was old, and I knew I was taking a chance.

This doctor searched for me at home and drove to places where I should be. He even went to the back alleys of Pine Ridge and to White Clay (Nebraska). He searched for me, because he knew very well, being a doctor, that this open wound might get infected and maybe even cause my death. So, he searched everywhere, and finally thought I might be at Wounded Knee. Under the strict supervision of the FBI, medical people were let through the roadblock to tend to the sick and carry in medicine, but that was all. They could not take foodstuffs in, only cough syrup and pills, and not much of these.

On the seventh day of Wounded Knee, Dr. Nodebaum went in with a medical team and had me searched out. We had called Dr. Lone Elk to come to Wounded Knee. I do not know the extent of his work at the Pine Ridge Indian Hospital, but he worked at the hospital at that time. Anyway, he knew me well because we are related. He found me sitting there in the basement of the church, and he said, "Your doctor wants you outside. He has come after you and wants to take you away."

When Dr. Nodebaum found me, he shook my hand. "We missed you," he said. I rode back with him to the Pine Ridge Indian Health Service Hospital and he personally tended to my wound. He cleansed the infected area, applied medicine, and bandaged it. When he was through and while I was putting my clothes on, he was sitting there on his high stool. When I was completely clothed, buttoning up my shirt and putting on my jacket, he got after me. I remember what he said.

"It is not for you to go into Wounded Knee. Look at all those others. Look outside on that road. There are young men walking that road who could be in Wounded Knee. Why are they home? For one thing, they are chicken. They do not want to go into Wounded Knee. They do not want to show themselves that they are Lakota. There are many of those people walking the streets and walking the highway, and some are at home. You are a very sick person. You should be at home because your health is your number one priority."

The doctor shook my hand again, and said, "I understand why you went in there. Because the people needed help, because the people were in trouble and suffering. You went in there to do your part. For this, I admire you." Afterward, Dr. Lone Elk drove me home to Mission Flat in his car.

It was good and yet it was sad to be home, knowing what I know of Wounded Knee 1973. It was sad knowing that people there were still hungry and cold. They stayed there because they wanted to, because they did not like the setup of the tribal council that lorded itself over the people. Knowing what Wounded Knee was really about made me sad to be home. I wished I was able-bodied and healthy. I would have stayed at Wounded Knee from its beginning to its finish.

The first Saturday after I returned home I went to the store to buy a few things. In the store, I met Jonas Walks Under the Ground. We know each other quite well. He came over and shook my hand. I was still a weak, sickly-looking person. He said, "I am glad to see you moving about. Try hard to get well. Tomorrow night we are going to have a peyote meeting (Native American Church), and I personally invite you to come." So I said, "I will. Since you invite me, I will be there." Upon reaching home, I told my wife, "I am invited to a peyote meeting." That Sunday night my wife took me to where Jonas and his wife, Suzy, were living. They were the ones who held the meeting.

The meeting, called the Peyote Way, is a ceremony that begins in the evening and continues throughout the night, until sunrise or later. I have been to these ceremonies before and I know just what to do. My wife drove me to this meeting and I told her, "Remain here, and when you see me enter the building, you can take off and go home. But, I want you to come back about eight o'clock tomorrow. I will want to go home then and lay down and rest. In this meeting, we have to sit up and so I will be overly tired. So come as early as you can, so that I can get home and go to bed and rest."

I went to the outside fireplace. No one was outside, but I knew that the fire chief, the person who tends to the fire, would come out. It was a chilly night, so I was warming myself when the fire chief came out. He recognized me, walked over, shook my hand, and asked me if I came for the meeting, and I said, "Yes." He said, "I will go in and talk to the leader," and then he went inside. After a while he came out. "It is very crowded in there, but I have made a space beside where I am sitting and you can sit there."

We started toward the building, and I waved to my wife for her to go.

Around midnight, when the drum stopped, the leader, Ira Elk Boy, spoke. He said, "We have a new attendee here, just arrived, and we know that he was in Wounded Knee. Many of you attending this meeting have relatives in Wounded Knee, so I want him to talk a little about the conditions in Wounded Knee." In the silence of that crowded room, I talked about Wounded Knee. I told them how conditions were. After my talk was over, the meeting resumed.

I stayed at the meeting all the way through. After midnight, I was given a chance to pray out loud. In that prayer, I implored the Great Spirit, Wakan Tanka, to bless the people at Wounded Knee, to give them courage and strength, and to help them. Some had families at home, and some had children at home attending school who were left in the care of relatives. I was very grateful that they gave me a special invitation to attend this meeting so that I could pray for those who were in Wounded Knee.

The eyes and ears of the whole world were focused on Wounded Knee, and this is one reason why the Marshals, the FBI, and Wilson's goons did not rush into Wounded Knee to annihilate the Lakotas who were there like they did in 1890. They did not kill the spirit of Wounded Knee 1890, and they did not kill the spirit of Wounded Knee 1973. There is unrest and there is misunderstanding causing misery for Native Americans, but the spirit of the Lakota shall go on as long as Wakan Tanka, the Great Spirit, watches over us.

>>>→ • ←<<<

Many tribes, even our neighbors the Mexicans, found their way into Wounded Knee. And from all directions—north, south, east, and west—local people took time out to guide people in who had never been in Wounded Knee. When people wished to leave, the local people who knew the terrain led them out. They knew the ways to get around the roadblocks, and the ways to hide when the flares were lit. At one point during my stay in Wounded Knee, a heavy bomber came from the south. All the men who had firearms, which were mainly .22s, fired at the bomber. No matter how small the weaponry or how unequal in numbers, when facing the forces of a mighty opposition the fight in the heart of the Lakota was strong.

I am glad that I spent just seven days and seven nights in Wounded Knee 1973. I am glad I did my bit. When the two Red Clouds were asked to help out in our misery and did not show up, they failed the people. Six of us were selected to do this work, and they were the only two who did not show up. How can we look to them to be leaders of this Sioux Nation? At Wounded Knee 1973, they showed they did not answer the call to help the people get over this trying time. I do not look to the Red Clouds as leaders. They might be smart in talking; they might even holler and be loud, but they did not show up in Wounded Knee 1973. That proves they are not leaders of the Lakota Nation.

Several times during this occupation, many people knew that Dick Wilson said, "I have my ninety guns that will march into Wounded Knee and wipe it out." What do you think about that? It would be a repetition of Wounded

Knee 1890—this time Dick Wilson's goons rather than the 7th Cavalry. I think it was clear, at least to a point, to the Marshals and the FBI that if Dick Wilson was allowed to do this, it would be known all over the world because of the press and television people. The BBC, ABC, NBC, CBS, and many others were inside Wounded Knee. They knew we had a lot of people talking of the conditions evident in Wounded Knee 1973.

Several books have been written about Wounded Knee, but I think that those people who were in Wounded Knee know for themselves that what is written in these books is not complete. I have stated what I thought about it in an Indian way. We have among us a certain percentage of the goons and their children that are still with us. The problem is still here. It will be here until the day the Great Spirit sees to it in His merciful love to change the way of life at the so-called end of the world.

I can still recall how it was at Wounded Knee in 1973. There were people from all over—Canada, the state of Washington, California, the Southwest. There was a great love there; we understood each other. We were hungry together, we were tired together, we were cold together. We know what brotherhood is because we lived it. We know the meaning of love. Buddy LaMont gave his life during the course of his stay in Wounded Knee 1973. Frank Clearwater, another Indian from a tribe out east, gave his life. There are others—a girl from Nova Scotia died.

Through the years after Wounded Knee 1973, some young men and women gave their lives for what happened in Wounded Knee. They were very special people. Pedro Bisonette was one of them. He was a leader of the Oglala Sioux civil rights organization. Anna Mae Aquash paid with her life, too. The Pine Ridge goons or the police murdered them; we know this. But the record on this says differently.

These wrongs will have to be answered and paid for; they are not forgiven. I do not think those people in Wounded Knee who were there and suffered in Wounded Knee 1973 have ever forgiven what the FBI, the Marshals, and Dick Wilson's goons have done to us. Before I said that forgiveness is one of the greatest acts of mercy, compassion, and love that any person can do. But our tradition and the beliefs that we live by, this heritage of ours since Wakan Tanka placed us here in this world, says that any Lakota who fires upon another Lakota is not Lakota, and shall never again be Lakota. For myself there is no forgiveness for this type of person. So, we know where we stand.

Are we Lakota or not? We are Lakota and nothing can change that. It is a way of life that Wakan Tanka, the Great Spirit, gave to us, and we understand that. We lived it, we suffered in it. This thought sings in the hearts of people who were in Wounded Knee in 1973. This cradle of life in which the Great Spirit protects us will continue for as long as this Earth is our Mother. And when the Great Spirit, in His merciful love, makes changes in this world that we always refer to as the end of the world, there will be an answering of the wrongs. The Lakota who fired upon another Lakota will have to answer. I do not care what kind of a religion they turn to in order to hide their bad conscience; they will answer for the bullets that they slung into the Indian encampment at Wounded Knee 1973.

The fires of Wounded Knee are still burning. They shall burn until the time when this Earth is changed altogether. They will burn in front of the face of the Great Spirit. We shall never forget those who have given their lives; we may forget their names, but their spirits are still here with us. They have come close to us; they have become our relations now and forever. This is the Lakota way—this is the tradition that we are accustomed to.

Atlanta, Georgia, 1990

Pete Catches was active in the civil rights movement during the same period as Dr. Martin Luther King, Jr. In his view, King was a "dog soldier," or a warrior who placed himself in harm's way to protect his people. In 1990 in Atlanta, Georgia, the King family adopted Pete, and in 1991, he was presented with the Martin Luther King Freedom Award in Washington, D.C.

Dr. Martin Luther King was a man whom I looked up to with deep respect as a man of the people. I would call Dr. King a true warrior and leader who put his life on the line to help the suffering and forgotten people of this world. I have stated before that Dr. Martin Luther King threw his lance into the ground on the battlefield, tethered himself to the lance, and vowed never to leave until the battle was won. And, as is the common fate of the greatest warriors and leaders of this world, he sacrificed his life for his people and his belief that the Creator put all of us here as equal human beings.

In the winter of 1989–1990, I was privileged to be among several Native American spiritual leaders and representatives invited to meet with board members and staff of the Martin Luther King Center for Nonviolent Social Change in Atlanta, Georgia, to discuss how the African American and Native American communities could work together to resolve problems of mutual concern, including domestic issues and the global issue of achieving world peace. The meeting took place during King Week 1990, the celebration of his sixty-first birthday and the fifth national holiday honoring Dr. King. I was put in the position of being elder statesman and spiritual leader for the Native American assemblage. I never felt comfortable being put in this kind of position; I feel better being at the back, just being part of the group. I was asked to tape a message for the Indian students at Cemawa Indian School in Oregon, and to speak at the ecumenical services on Dr. King's birthday.

I have been invited back to the Center and to be a part of the King family. This experience is something in my life that I never thought would happen, even in my dreams. I will be steadfast in my support of everyone associated with the King Center. I want to do my best to live up to my commitment. My prayers will always be with Coretta Scott King and all the King family.

MESSAGE TO CEMAWA INDIAN STUDENTS

I have a good feeling that this day is special, a memorial to Dr. Martin Luther King, Jr., and his philosophy and ideas in life. It should go all over the world, especially to young people. This being a special day, I want to impart unto you a blessing of the Great Spirit, to let you understand and see what is good and beautiful in life, and that in your life you will adhere to good principles, the things that will manifest themselves into something to help other people walk the Red Road of Life.

As young students, you have the great opportunity to grow up into a strong generation, a generation that will be smarter than the previous generation. The same is also true of the generations behind you. This is called tradition, a heritage given to us by the Great Spirit. We must keep it alive, we must work hard, and we must help each other.

I do not see you now, but in my mind, I can picture every one of you. This is the work of the Great Spirit. I am talking directly to you, hoping that you will grasp something from this message and carry on that banner, or that torch, or that idea. We are in a march for peace. And in order to get that peace, we must love one another. We must work together to see each other, not in color, not in culture, but as true brothers of one family under God. It will be a hard road for some of us. But, the effort must be there. It will be hard sometimes to stay on the right path, but remember always that the Great Spirit is beside you.

The answers to problems throughout our lives are within all of us. They are lying there dormant; we have to stir them up. We have to seek the answers to the problems that assail us. And in that way, knowing this, knowing that the Great Spirit is with us, we can surely and truly be a part of a movement for world peace.

We all have a job to do. We should not leave anything unturned to do that job and to put our efforts together. I see in all of you the resemblance of Christ because He is in us, and we are in Him. Let the goodness that is in you shine. Continue that way, ever bright, full of love, so beautiful, as part of His Creation. Look around you and enjoy His creation—the daylight, the stars at night, the moon, the sun, the air. All this is beautiful. Use it well.

Do not revert to alcohol and drugs. Stay away from them. Whenever you have an urge to resort to alcohol and drugs, think of this old man who has experienced drunkenness. This man was a drunk himself at one time, but who has come away and committed his entire life, the remaining portion of his life, to sobriety. You, too, can do that.

You are beautiful. Whatever is in you is beautiful. Live with it. Enjoy the things that are around you, the food that you eat, the water that you drink, the air that you breathe. As you gaze in the far distant horizon, see the lightning and hear the thunder, the voice of the Great Spirit. He is that close to you. When you walk, you walk on the bosom of our Mother, the Earth.

So today, I am privileged to say these very few words, words of love, for you. May the Great Spirit bless you. May His love shine upon you and guide you through life, direct you, make you strong, make you love one another. Because love is a tool for peace. We have to have love first, love of our neighbor, to know what peace is. We cannot have peace with Star Wars. We cannot have peace through the conquest of minorities. We can have peace in no other way than to love one another. The Christmas message the angels brought—peace on earth, good will to men—is not only intended for Christmas time. It is meant for all of our lives, every day of our lives. And we must strive to keep in mind the principles that are so valuable, the virtues that are ever present that we can use—honesty and truthfulness, love for one another, obedience, long suffering, perseverance. These are values that we have to live by and share with each other. This is love.

Love comes in many ways. Love is not just when you kiss one another. You love the flowers, you love the running streams, you love the mountains, and you love the sunshine and the chill of the winter wind. This is love. We are part of nature. So, let us be one with nature. The way the Great Spirit created nature was beautiful in all its goodness. The streams were running pure and clean; the mountaintops with their snowcaps were pure. With all the factories, the rivers are now polluted—the fish drift downstream, their lives gone because of pollution. We can change this. The Great Spirit created this universe.

We have come to an age where we have to stand together and understand each other in order to help each other. We ask ourselves, "How can I be of help to others?" You can be a role model whatever age you are, whether you are a teenager, or in your twenties or thirties. You do not have to advertise, "I do not drink alcohol, I do not use drugs." You do not have to say that. You can live it and people will notice. They will see that you are living a good life. They will see that you go out of your way to do things that are right. They will understand you. They will love you for that. And I think that living this way is the Red Road of Life.

When you get up in the morning, the first thought that enters your mind should be one of thankfulness that you awoke on another beautiful day. Be thankful that you are privileged to enjoy another day. When food is on the table, be thankful that you are able to eat some of it. When you take a drink of water, bless yourself with this water, because water, too, is sacred. There is no living thing that can stay alive without water. Water is so important that when we partake of it and drink some, we respect it. Our love touches it.

In our daily lives, we should continue with utmost care to be role models. I know that sometimes it is going to be hard to do this. I should know at my age. Some days seem dreary and bleak. But look around you. The old medicine man who taught me said this: "Look to nature, because nature will teach you. The power of the earth, the power of the sea, two separate things, each has its own separate power. We are part of that, the cycle that we live. The water that flows down the river will return some day. It will flow to the ocean, and it will go up into the atmosphere and in the form of rain and snow, come back to us again."

So, too, life is a cycle. We begin at birth, we continue to live a complete life, and when we get to old age, we arrive back where we started. We become feebleminded, losing our sight, our hearing, and our teeth. If we become too aged, we crawl on all fours like the babies we were at one time. This is life. It revolves in a cycle. From where it began, we arrive back to that place. We come from the Great Spirit through Mother Earth, and to Her we shall return some day.

Before we return to Mother Earth, we have this life to live. Why not live this life in the goodness of the Great Spirit the way He meant for us to live, in a beautiful environment in a beautiful way. We can do it. I know you can do it. It is in you to do what needs to be done. And I am sure, guided by the Great Spirit, His blessing and His grace, you can live a good life and be role models, whatever age you are. In this fashion, others will follow you. You need to plant the seed. You need to grow into that model.

I will close here with a prayer that will include all of you, in my own tongue, in my own way, as the Great Spirit intended me to pray. So, I leave you with a great love in my heart for you. May the Great Spirit love you, bless you in everything that you do, in every way that you wish to live your future life.

ECUMENICAL SERVICES

I love every one of you. I came here because I wanted to. Yesterday I had planned to direct a memorial ceremony on the Rosebud Reservation. I was given notice of the ceremony quite a while beforehand, but I chose to come here. It is important that I would be among you today on this sixty-first birthday and holiday celebration of Dr. Martin Luther King, Jr., that the flower of freedom will include the red race, this beautiful flower of His creation.

The flower of freedom began with one root and now it is becoming united with other roots to form a single cause—the march of freedom. Just as the walls of Eastern Europe and elsewhere have shaken and fallen down, so too may the walls of misunderstanding and of poverty be shaken and crumble and fall, to unite all of us in one family, in one beautiful flower as the Lord intended it to be.

That flower is the flower of love. That flower is the flower of understanding. It is so pure that its perfume will ascend throughout the whole world with the blessing of the Great Spirit, the Lord of all people and nations. I will pray now.

Petaga Yuha Mani conducting a ceremony outside the initi, 1982.

Four *(Topa)*
CEREMONIES

Inipi (Purification), The First Form of Prayer

I think that the name "sweat lodge" is not the proper name for
this sacred rite. We should not devalue the rite with a common
word like "sweat." Of course, we do sweat in a sweat lodge, but
the proper name for the rite is Inipi (Purification).

As oral history points out to us, the Purification Rite
is the oldest form of prayer of the Native aboriginals in
North America. Included are people in Mexico, the fifty
states, and Canada. In my travels to many states, I have
come upon Alaskan Eskimos who enjoy going into a sweat
lodge with us. Being Natives, the original inhabitants of
this Western Hemisphere, the sweat lodge is the first form
of prayer that Natives know in seeking the Great Spirit's
blessing and help.

The sweat lodge, so to speak, is very important to us.
I see the Purification Rite as very important in the life of
the Lakota people, especially for those who have anything
to do with the Pipe. Purification of body, mind, and spirit
is important for those who want Pipe ceremonies, go to the

Sundances, have naming ceremonies for their children, doctor members of their family, or the ceremony after losing someone who has gone from this world into the next. Purification, or the sweat lodge, is necessary so that the Great Spirit will come to the occasion and bless our happy and sad ceremonies, our Pipe, our prayers, our lives.

Whenever weather permits, we should go into the Purification Rite, because, when we purify ourselves—bodies, minds, and spirits—we can come close to the Great Spirit. We know He loves us. He created us. He fashioned this world for us. He wants us to live this way. He gave us these rites. Through these rites we can talk to Him, implore and ask Him favors, and receive a healing, receive help for the things we are troubled with. To me, the sweat lodge is so powerful, so good, so lovely, so in peace. You will experience peace in the sweat lodge.

My trailer camp is a poor place, situated nine miles north of Pine Ridge on Highway 18, going toward Hot Springs, and off to the left about a half mile. On a little table of land stands a small trailer that people pull behind a pickup truck or a car. Until heavy summer winds toppled it, we had what is known as a squaw cooler, a shade made of pine boughs. Just a few yards south of the squaw cooler is my sweat lodge, fenced in with woven wire. Because I respect the area immediately around my sweat lodge, dogs and cats are not allowed near the area; everyone knows that dogs will pee on anything. In my mind long years ago, I decided that when I set up a sweat lodge I would fence it with woven wire to keep dogs and cats away so that the

Tunkasilas, the Tunkan, the rocks that are to be used, will not be desecrated. The wood to be used in the fire pit and the canvas over the frame of the sweat lodge are also protected. But most of all, I want to protect that little mound of dirt in front of the opening of the sweat lodge, which is especially sacred to me. Even when I just go and clean my fire pit of ashes, I stop at the gate and look over the area and check to see that all is well.

As I mentioned before, we have strong winds through there, and my sweat lodge covering is scattered here and there, torn from its frame. It can probably stand one more year. The canvas and the rugs lie on the ground. The snow and the rain have frozen them to the ground and they could not be straightened out, so I left them that way. But the frame is intact. The reverence, the thought of a sacred place still lingers there. My wife takes her tobacco there, places it in the sweat lodge, and prays. Even though over these many months the rocks in the center from the last sweat lodge have gone cold since the first snow, we still touch the rocks with reverence. When we offer our tobacco ties and our Bull Durham, we touch the stones.

Toward the setting sun further west from the entrance of the sweat lodge and the mound, is the fire pit. The fire pit signifies an old man, shaped like a horseshoe or a face. When you clean the fire pit of ashes, sprinkle them along the outer edges. After you have sweat lodge ceremonies a dozen or more times, you will see the semblance of an old man, graying hair, dark in places, but mostly gray. Mother Earth and that old man, which is the fire of life, go together, hand in hand on this Red Road of Life. Around the fire pit, you sprinkle ashes of the last used fire pit, a constant reminder that we shall return to dust at the end of our lives.

PREPARATIONS

Long ago when the old-timers went out to gather sage in preparation for a sweat lodge, they would bring back huge armfuls of sage. They did not make just one trip. They would go on foot, way out on the plains where the sage is fresh and pure. They would bring it back and put a mat on the ground inside the sweat lodge. The more time you put into preparing a sweat lodge, the better. Every breath that you take while you are working there is a prayer. The thoughts that you have while you are working are a part of the prayer. Every step, every motion that you undertake, is part of the prayer of the sweat lodge to be held.

The old-timers would bring back two rocks, walking back every step. In the old days, the Indians took *wasa* (red paint made from clay) with them. They prayed and then painted the rocks that they were going to take home. They talked to the rocks because at one time, ages and ages ago, Wakan Tanka made them. The rocks might have been very big, even as big as a house, but over time became small. But through those rocks, the prayers will be bigger than a house, maybe big enough to bring health to some person. One person made several trips carrying two rocks at a time, and placed the rocks near the fire pit. Then they would go into the woods, cut wood there, and haul it back by carrying it on their shoulders. This is how it was done.

In this day and age people drive out in pickups, gather the sage, the rocks, and the wood all in one shot. They might even bring back thirty, forty, fifty rocks, half a pickup truck load of wood, and a whole bunch of sage. And while doing this, they will have a cigarette in their mouths. That is not reverence for the Purification Rite that is being prepared. I see this often, and I have spoken against it.

The sacred Pipe must be filled before a sweat lodge ceremony. The Pipe will be brought in and smoked during the ceremony. The true way to fill a Pipe is to begin by singing the Pipe-filling song. When the medicine man offers this pinch of tobacco to the West and prays, he prays for the people entering the sweat lodge, their families, and whatever their needs may be. He offers tobacco to the Four Directions, to Wanble Gleska (Spotted Eagle), and to Mother Earth. When he is through filling the Pipe, he stands up with it and offers it to the Four Directions, to the Heavens above, and to our Mother the Earth.

In order for it to be a good ceremony, when you fill the Pipe, you should pray in the Lakota tongue, the native tongue that Wakan Tanka gave to us. The English language should not be used because it is foreign, belonging to other people somewhere else. The Lakota way is the Red Road of Life. Only if we do them correctly will He bless our ceremonies, will He answer our prayers.

Participant in Inipi carrying tunka.

INSIDE THE SWEAT LODGE

I see many mistakes by "modern" Indians in conducting a sweat lodge ceremony. When you go into a sweat lodge ceremony, you must close your lips. Nowadays, even at Sundance sweat lodges, some people joke inside of a sweat lodge. An old man, about whom I will speak later, told me this: "The rocks have no eyes; they have no ears, they have no mouths. But they see you, they hear you. They echo your prayer to the Great Spirit. So, when the spirits are there, you should sit there with reverence, reverence for yourself, respect for yourself, and respect to be one of the honored participants of a sweat lodge ceremony. A person should be silent. They should sit there in silent devotion when the rocks are brought in."

When a medicine man begins praying, and when he sings a song, we should support him and sing along. Even when we do not know the song, we should hum, following his tune. In order to be perfect, in order to have power, we must become as one. We must all work together. If only half of the people in the sweat lodge are enthused in a ceremony, and the other half have their minds on something else, such as women, money, jobs, things other than what is taking place, the rite is only half as powerful as it could be. When everyone, all of the people in a sweat lodge, go along and work together and pray together, then they are one—solid and strong—to implore the Great Spirit for His love so that He will take care of us.

When the Pipe is brought in after two door openings, I often see individuals sitting there going through

the motions of pointing to the Four Directions, to
Mother Earth, touching the rocks, and killing a lot of
time. The medicine man has already done that. So, when
the Pipe is to be smoked inside, why should everyone sit
there and be motioning to the Four Directions, to the
rocks, and to whatever? That is not necessary; it has
already been done.

I could go on and on talking about the sweat lodge, the
Purification Rite, but I see so many mistakes in many places
that I have visited. In some places where I was invited to a
sweat lodge ceremony, some of them come out after each
door opening because they cannot stand the heat, and they
go back in before it is shut tight again. I feel that this is
wrong. I think that when you enter a sweat lodge before the
ceremony starts, you should remain in there until the conclusion and then come out. The Purification Rite to me is a
sacred ceremony, a solid way of prayer, in part, because it
involves suffering.

I know that what I am saying here seems not right to
some other tribes. I respect their ways of conducting a sweat
lodge. I have heard that in certain places, the sweat lodge
door is opened seven times. I think this is a beautiful practice, because we have Seven Sacred Rites (Purification Rite,
Pipefast, Sundance, Making of a Relative, Coming of Age,
Releasing of the Spirit, and Throwing of the Ball). In the
Spotted Eagle's Way, the sweat lodge entrance doorway faces
the west. Sweat lodge doorways are different according to
the sacred rites of other medicine men (bear, elk, the *yuwipi*,
and so on)—toward the east, north, south—and even a door-

way in the ceiling of the sweat lodge. But in the Spotted Eagle Pipe Way, the sweat lodge doorway faces the west.

Because we do things differently, we are weak. If all of us unite and do things in the same way, with one mind, one language, and one song, while also praying together, we will be loved by the Great Spirit and become strong. This is the Pipe Way: whoever uses the Pipe in the proper way, honoring it, cherishing it, loving it, living with it, taking care of it, and thinking that it is a priceless gift, He will give to us whatever our needs may be. No matter how many horses, cars, or homes we may have, the Pipe is far more precious.

GOOD LANCE'S TEACHINGS

The old one (Good Lance) who taught me this medicine way of life told me this: "These rocks that you call Tunkan have no eyes, have no ears, and have no mouths, but it is through these that we pray to the Great Spirit. When we enter a sweat lodge, these same rocks implore the Great Spirit to see us, they hear our prayer, and they implore the Great Spirit to receive our prayer. They are the intercessors. Through the heat of the sweat lodge, the rocks bring the prayer of the Lakota to the Great Spirit."

Good Lance also told me that the dirt mound in front of the entrance of the sweat lodge is a huge mountain. We see a dirt pile, maybe twelve inches high. But when the spirits come, the supernatural, this little pile of dirt is like a mountain. The top of this little dirt pile reaches into the heavens, into the world beyond, into the domain of the Great Spirit.

≫→ • ←≪

The old man beckoned me to go with him as he was going to tell me something. He said, "Little brother, this little mound of dirt that you can step over in this physical world, there are many good men and good women who could not go to the top, to the summit, of this small mound of dirt. In the supernatural spirit way, this mound reaches into the heavens and beyond, into the domain of the Great Spirit. Little brother, whatever you do, strive to get to that summit. You have all your life to climb it, and someday you will stand on the pinnacle of this summit, of this huge mountain that rises above this vast world.

"There are many good men and many good women who just go part way, and stumble and fall all the way down. There is a route, a path, known as the Pipe Trail. There is a path, the same path, that is known as the medicine way of life—curing the sick, helping those who have problems and who are in need. If you follow that path, someday you will reach the top. In the effort to get to the top, some are overly anxious and they tumble down, clear down to the base and beyond. Their second effort is much harder than the first. Even, little brother, if you have to crawl on your belly, using your elbows to crawl up that huge mountain, do so. Even if you skin your elbows, even if there are tears in your eyes, even if your tribulations are so heavy that they try to pull you down to this earth that we are so accustomed to, try...try.... And in the effort of trying, you may even shed tears. Up on the summit someday, the Great Spirit will accept your Pipe, if you use it right.

"The path of this Pipe Way and medicine way is your Lakota way of life—your language, your way, your culture, your tradition, your heritage. You have to speak Lakota. This is the way, the Red Road of Life. The beginning is the sweat lodge ceremony, and all through your life you will have to follow that path, the Red Road of Life."

The talk of the Pipe Way, Cannunpa Tawooglake, says this: "Whosoever respects this Pipe, honors it, takes care of it, loves it, will have a long life. He will one day walk with three legs (meaning walk with a cane), and if he continues to live that beautiful way of life, even though his eyesight is gone, his teeth are gone, his ears are no more, he may walk like an animal with four legs, using two canes.

"The Pipe Way is a beautiful way, and it is a hard way. There are many difficult times along the way, that long journey up the hill where good men and good women topple and roll down to the base."

Good Lance told me that someday I would understand. It was perhaps five or six years after he left this world that I understood what he told me that day about the little hill in front of the doorway of the sweat lodge.

One must love all of the sweat lodge—the frame, the coverings, the little pile of dirt in front of the doorway, and the fire pit. Good Lance also told me, "Do not leave the fire pit, because the fire, the air, the water, and the earth are four of the most essential things of life, and this is part of the Lakota prayer. Around the fireplace is health. Around the fireplace is a new rebirth, children coming into the world. Around the fire pit is a place that you should go, whether there is a fire in it in preparation for a sweat lodge, or whether you get up early in the morning and walk to the sweat lodge area. Go to the fire pit and look around; see the old man looking at you, a constant reminder that we have one life, that some day our hair will be as white as what we are seeing." So, I do this. It is a beautiful way of life, a way that is the beginning of any Lakota ceremony.

A WAY OF LIFE

Earlier I mentioned that the Lakota religion is very unique, a thing apart, not like the other religions where they have a membership drive and things like that. We can go to a sweat lodge ceremony and partake of the ceremony, and then, we can stay away for an entire year, or two or three. According to circumstances, a person might be at work, he might be under contract somewhere, or he might be in a foreign country where sweat lodges are not known. He might be away for five or six years, but when he comes back, he can go to a sweat lodge. He is as welcome to go there as the first time that he went.

When walking the pathway, the Red Road of Life, we should do it right each day to our utmost ability, to be certain that what we do is right and aboveboard, nothing hidden, nothing sneaky, nothing underhanded. The Great Spirit fashioned the path and gave it to us. He sees everything we do, what we think in the sweat lodge, and how we pray. He decides whether it shall grow. Shall He bless the prayers that we say? Shall He bless us, bless our ceremony?

Lakota religion is like a tree, one type of tree, the Tree of Life that Wakan Tanka planted. Its roots are there in a sweat lodge. Its foundation is the rocks in the center, tempered with heat, tempered with prayer, tempered with sacred songs. And as it grows, it glows red, like the color of the fire. And how we live, using the sweat lodge in our lives, is the way that tree will ascend before Wakan Tanka, for Him to see what our lives were really like.

What I have tried to explain here is the Red Road of Life, about respect for the sweat lodge, the deep devotion that we should have when we go into a sweat lodge. When we enter a sweat lodge, we have to focus our minds. The prayers that we say must be in Lakota. When the White Buffalo Calf Woman brought the sacred Pipe to the Sioux people many centuries ago, she did not bring it to an English-speaking people. The Creator, Wakan Tanka, brought the Pipe to a Lakota-speaking people and that is how it is meant to be.

I am not saying that non-Indians should not go to a sweat lodge. It is my belief that those white people who go to the sweat lodge ceremonies were, in their former lives, Natives themselves, because we strongly believe in reincarnation. The only thing is that, if they want to continue in this Indian ceremonial way, attend sweat lodges, go on a Pipefast and be a part of a Sundance, they should learn Lakota. I repeat, I do not care if they are white people. If they want to Sundance, if they want to Pipefast, if they want to take part in the sweat lodge ceremony, they should learn Lakota, and I do not mean maybe. Absolutely! It is easy to learn the language. When you learn the Lakota language, you know that you have entered into the realm of a unique religion, a religion that is very beautiful and of the Western Hemisphere.

It did not come from overseas. It was from this Western Hemisphere that the Lakota religion transpired.

When we go to any kind of a ceremony—a Pipe ceremony, a Pipefast, a Sundance, wedding, funeral, naming ceremony, or whatever—we should first go into a sweat lodge to purify our minds, our spirits, and our physical beings, to be able to stand barefooted in a sacred area, fill our Pipes, and pray to the Great Spirit, and we will be certain that He will be there. We will be certain that He will bless us, that He will hear us, that whatever we ask of Him may come to pass.

TALKING TO THE HOLY STONES
By Peter V. Catches (Zintkala Oyate)

The healer fills the sacred Pipe. He beckons toward the west, north, east, and south, to the heavens, then to our nourishing Mother Earth. All this while the Pipe filling song is sung.

The medicine man enters the ancient spiritual womb of this sacred rite. Here we cleanse our impurities, heal our age-old wounds, and begin to grow, love, and forgive. He enters uttering a simple mitakuye oyasin (for all my relations). We do the same as we follow him in.

The healer motions and Tunkan (the Grandfathers) are brought in and set in the west, then the north, east, and south, toward the heavens, and finally our Mother Earth. The final, and seventh, Grandfather (Tunka) is to help us help ourselves.

The water is brought in and all of us grip the rim of the container. The healer invokes the blessing from ancient oral tradition. We acknowledge and submit to its sacredness. The time has come, the time is now, it has begun. In spirit and in prayer we have begun as one.

The door is closed. Although there are many in this sacred place, each one of us is alone. A four-direction song is sung with the medicine man in the lead. Someone is beating a drum; it helps. Water is poured on the Tunkan; the steam is everywhere.

The spirit-calling song is sung with respectful love. The person sitting across from the healer begins his prayer. We support his prayer and feel his need and we give it hope. Individual prayers continue in a clockwise direction, each ending with "mitakuye oyasin." The space in the holy wheel of prayer has come to me.

"Great Mystery, Grandfather, look this way. There is nothing holy in and around this place, only that which You have touched and it became holy. I send this voice, its plea spoken from my heart, and it is my spirit's choice.

"I know from the concourses of the avenue of light that through the Grandfathers You can hear my thoughts. My love for You is here, and I have no doubts. In doing so You have made the words of this prayer holy.

"This plea is to ensure that I do not forget we are all related, that I am here as part of Your perfect design, that the path I will follow is of love and growth. I admit and acknowledge that I sometimes become weak and succumb to vices that are virtueless and thus harm myself more.

>>>—→ • ←—<<<

SACRED FIREPLACE

"It is then that I crawl here to find out what has gone wrong and You are always here. I love You, Great Spirit. Mitakuye oyasin."

There are a few more prayers, and a couple more songs are sung. The healer says the word for the door to open. As the door opens, the hot air rushes out and cool air slowly comes in. We all sit silently in sincere reverence. This is how the generations before us have acted, listening to the sounds coming from the Grandfathers. It is said, and I believe that any individual who is prepared and understands can hear the Grandfathers talking, that he or she can hear old songs that become new as if reborn.

The medicine man looks at every individual to see and feel if anything is wrong. He has the power to let you continue or release you from this prayer. He finds that all is one and he motions for the door to close a second time.

The healer is praying in the ancient language. We are not listening, because we are singing the song of compassion, the song of love, and the song of unity. There is an upsurge of emotional energy expanding outward in me. There is no fear in me now; I do not understand the word. The intense heat numbs my senses and it's as if I am a song, a song building my love for Wakan Tanka. I am joy, I am happy, I am someone. The medicine man shouts "Mitakuye oyasin," and the door opens.

There is a long silence. You can hear the breaths of relief as normal air replaces the hot, steamy moisture of this spiritual place in this sacred rite.

When the medicine man motions, the doorman walks to the fire to retrieve a small dry limb that has been placed there for this purpose. He takes the bowl of the sacred Pipe in his left hand and kneels in the doorway. He begins to puff on the Pipe with the burning limb stationed above the rim of the bowl. The cansasa (or *kinnikinnick*) ignites and smoke comes.

The Pipe journeys from person to person, received from the right and passed to the left. It comes to me; I clasp it with firm hands and gently puff from the stem. I repeat what is in my heart. The smoke enters my body as an incense to clear the cocoon of my spirit, to open the wings of my prayer, the words of my love spiraling forth in purity. I pass it on by saying, "mitakuye oyasin."

The medicine man finishes the sacred Pipe and sends it out. He motions to the doorman as he fills the dipper with the blessed water. It is now medicine for the spirit and the doorman takes a sip and passes it on in the same manner as the Pipe; not one drop is spilled.

The motion is made and the door is closed for the third time. The healer says, "I do not speak in English in this sacred place. Those of you who speak our ancient language know what has transpired in the first two rounds, that we are here in our journey to the center of this beautiful prayer. We have cried together, prayed together, sung together, and watered the flower of our growth in understanding. For life to continue, it must embrace that love in your heart, to know that you have gained a treasure you alone know to be true. Now I return to my language."

There are three ending songs and all of us shout "mitakuye oyasin" and the door is opened. There is a long silence. I feel a tingling all over my body. I still feel the presence of the spirits, the helpers of this Spotted Eagle medicine man. I have gained understanding of my burdens so that I can deal with them effectively, now that I know I am not alone.

The door is closed for the last time. The healer's helpers have left and we cleanse ourselves for the last time. All of us get ready to reenter the realm of the living. The blessed water is returned to the Grandfathers and we are happy. I feel joy of life and I shout the songs in echoing gaiety, for my love of the Great Spirit will never end. From my heart I send this thanksgiving song:

> *Wakan Tanka wopila ecece ye ye lo.*
> *Wakan Tanka wopila ecece ye ye lo.*
> *Wakan Tanka wopila ecece ye lo hey ho.*
> *Cannunpa wan yuha wacece la*
> *unko amayalupta ca pilamaya ya ya lo.*
> *Wakan Tanka wopila ecece ye lo hey.*[12]
> *Mitakuye oyasin.*

> Great Mystery, I thank you.
> Great Mystery, I thank you.
> Great Mystery, I thank you.
> With this sacred Pipe, I have asked you
> and you have answered; I thank you.
> Great Mystery, I thank you.
> For all my relations.

The door opens, and we leave.

>»→ • ←«<

Hanbleceya (Pipefast)

The Pipe Way is the path of the sacred Red Road of Life. Without it, we cannot walk the sacred Red Road of Life. It has a language of its own, the Cannunpa Tawooglake. I cannot translate that, because when you translate it, it is all wrong. When you pray with the Pipe, you have to use Lakota, because the English language can mean so many different things. English is a deceptive language. They (the spirits) hear it in a certain way, but the man saying it could mean an altogether different thing. The Lakota language is true, and does not have curse words. The only bad word in the Lakota language is the word "bad."

Hanbleceya, or the Pipefast, is one of the sacred rites given to our people, and to me, it is a most beautiful prayer. It is unique and apart from the rest, even though all the other sacred rites given to us are beautiful. I think the Pipefast, the Hanbleceya, is truly the way I would pray to the Great Spirit, because no one is there to hear you. You stand out there in the heat of the day, wherever the selected place is, and pray for, say, one day and one night, or two days and two nights, or three days and three nights, or the whole four days and four nights. You cannot go beyond four days and four nights.

There is an Indian saying that whatever you do, do so with your heart in it. If you exceed that, there is such a thing as overdoing it. Then there is such a thing as not doing enough. We have to keep that in mind.

When we pledge to go through a Pipefast, we are not saying things that we can change later on. If we say we are going to go on a Pipefast for four days and four nights, we must under no circumstances change the number of days. We have to go four days and four nights, because regardless of who you are—king, queen, president of the United States—you should not tell the Great Spirit you will do something one way and then slack off, or do it another way. When you talk to the Great Spirit on selecting a day, you have to do exactly what you have told Him; otherwise, the Pipefast is nothing at all, it is just time wasted. It is crucial for the Pipefast to be precise, even if one has to go through the heat of the day, the cold of the night, the wind, the rain, the hail, and whatever else.

In preparing for a Pipefast, you have to do certain things. First, you have to prepare your Pipe. In the old Indian world, when people wanted to go on a fast, they prepared their own Pipes with their own hands. They did not go to a museum or an arts and crafts store, and buy a Pipe that is already made. I will tell you why. Do you know who made that Pipe? Do you know their history? Maybe it was a drunk who commercializes Pipes and is just selling them to buy more alcohol. Maybe that kind of person made the Pipe that you may have bought. You have to be very careful because you will be going into the presence of the Great Spirit.

You have to be vitally certain to do things right, and do them with your heart in the doing. In the old days, they had to fashion their Pipes from Pipe stones. They had to seek and acquire a chunk of Pipe stone, and they would fashion it. They did not sit there day and night until it was done. They worked on it, and they set it aside and did other chores that

needed to be done, such as chopping wood, looking for horses, cutting hay, putting up hay, repairing a root cellar, and
other daily life activities. When I say looking for horses, I am
speaking of the Indian world fifty or sixty years ago.

Sometimes at night when the family is quiet—when
the children and the man's wife are all asleep—then he would
sit alone and get to fashioning that Pipe stone. When he has
fashioned the stone, he would wait until the middle of winter to get the Pipe stem because at any other time of the year,
a piece of wood made into a Pipe stem would crack. In the
middle of the winter, all the sap in the tree drains into the
ground, so there is less chance of a piece of wood cracking.

Long ago the Pipefast was seen as a fearful thing. It is
not something that young bucks today like to do. Without
preparing, they buy a Pipe somewhere or even borrow one
somewhere. The Pipe that you use is supposed to be yours,
and you have to fashion it with loving care. It has to become
a part of you.

You would also need a pail, a knife, a wooden bowl, a
buffalo skull, and, if possible, sweetgrass. You have to have
cansasa (Indian tobacco), not the kind that you buy in a plas-
tic bag. You have to fashion the cansasa yourself by going
into the canyons and along the creeks, gathering the cansasa,
drying it, crumbling it, scraping it, and then adding the medicine that goes with it.

The rest of the things needed for a Pipefast are flags
for the four directions, a tobacco pouch fence to enclose
the area where the person is to fast, and a sleeping bag. In
the old Indian world, a man would take a buffalo robe with

him on a Pipefast. Nowadays, people take sleeping bags, which I approve of, because a person needs to sleep. When asleep, a person may receive answers to his prayers, or dream a sacred dream.

Fashioning the Pipe and getting the other things together would perhaps take three months. In the meantime, the person would speak with a medicine man whom he has chosen to help him. The medicine man would advise him on certain things and what to do.

When you have everything ready, you must prepare yourself, typically for an entire year. If you are prone to anger, you must stop. If you always have bad thoughts of others or if you are a womanizer, you must get these behaviors out of your system. If money has you by the nose and leads you around, get that out of your system. I know that many young men and women are junkies on alcohol, on *peji* (marijuana), or other drugs. These people will require two years of preparation to get the junk out of their systems.

You must get your interior prepared, because you are going to pray to the Great Spirit. When all is in readiness, you pray with these things that you have made ready, and you put them away with loving care. You take care of them until the proper time when you are ready to go on a Pipefast.

Again, always remember that you must do whatever you told the Great Spirit you would do. If you say two days and two nights, do not change it to three or four, and vice versa. You may fool yourself, you may fool your fellow man, you may even try to fool the medicine man, but you can never ever fool the Great Spirit. If you change your days, if you told the Great Spirit what you would do and then changed it, how do you expect Him to answer you when you pray to Him? You fooled around with Him, so He in turn will fool around with you. It is as simple as that.

Through the years that I have helped young men and women go on a Pipefast, I have seen all kinds of weather. One young man whom I placed in Rosebud country went three days and three nights, and the entire time it rained. What does the medicine man do? Is there some mistake? That is a good question; I do not know.

I can only say that you should remember that whatever you are seeking, the elements controlled by Wakan Tanka will make it worthwhile. If it rains all the way through, if on your second day a hailstorm comes, you should not run from that sacred area (which many people have done). Take it. You have the necessary ability in your mind to overcome the problem that wants to wrest you away from that sacred area. If you believe in this Wakan Tanka, come hail or high water (literally), you will remain there and pray to Him.

The Indian prayer in the Pipe Way was very unique. I remember years and years ago when I used to drink, I would go to church with a terrible hangover. But here, in this Lakota prayer, you cannot do that. You have to be honest with yourself; you have to clean your system because Wakan Tanka will be present where you will go.

I know of one young lady who went on a Pipefast for three days and three nights. She was sitting in a sweat lodge. Every time I approached her, every time I went to check on her, she would be crying. I said nothing, I just noticed that she was crying. Afterward she told me, "I looked at my life. I reviewed my life and asked myself, why am I sitting here?" I told her it was a good beginning, that she admitted in the presence of the Great Spirit how wrong her former life was, that Wakan Tanka loves her, that He blessed her, that she should continue on and acquire a Pipe and become a Pipe carrier. Her former life is over. A new life has begun, a lovely, beautiful way of life has begun. She is still in that way. She leads sweat lodge ceremonies, she does the praying, and she does the singing. Hanbleceya, as we know, is so beautiful, so strong, so lovely.

Let me tell you a story about Hanbleceya in that other Indian world. Around 1907, there was a young man who had a sacred dream and wanted to go on a Pipefast. He went to a medicine man and talked of his dream, and he asked the medicine man, "When can I present you with a Pipe to help me go through with this plan of Hanbleceya?" The medicine man said, "Anytime you feel like it, I will be willing to help you."

He went home and was talking to his father about it and his father said, "I will loan you my Pipe so that you can go and offer him the Pipe to help you. After you come back, you will have to fashion your own Pipe—the stone and the stem. You will have to get the things necessary together. You ask him what you need to have and he will tell you. Most of all, you take care of yourself. Clean yourself, make yourself good so that when you pray the Hanbleceya, the Great Spirit will listen to you."

In the ensuing months, the young man was lucky. He acquired a piece of Pipe stone. In the evenings he worked on it, fashioning the Pipe stone into the bowl. That winter he went out, got a stem, and fashioned that, too. He got the other things together, and so, by the time spring came around he was ready. He had prepared himself as well, and he went to several sweat lodge ceremonies.

They selected a day and he went on the fast. They put him out on the plains on the side of a hill. It is a sad story because he did not make it. He came back the very first night and he was sorry, he was sad. But, he said, "I will try again." So the following summer he tried again. They placed him at a different place and he came back again, he did not make it again. The third time they placed him in still another place and, once again, he did not make it. That is three times he failed to finish a Pipefast.

Since the young man failed three times, his father told him, "Go to that medicine man. He is very strict. Explain the situation, that you ran from the sacred area three times. Tell him that you want to be guided under him." The father and son wanted to make certain that he would go through with the fast the fourth time, because this was the final effort. If he failed in this one, he could not try again.

Anyway, the young man went to a strong medicine man and told him the situation, about his sacred dream, and that he tried to go on a fast for three summers in a row, and that every time he ran from the place. He said then, "I want you to do all you can to keep me there so that I would not be able to come away." So the medicine man accepted his Pipe, and said, "I will."

The day arrived for the final attempt at the fast. The medicine man rode a horse. The young man going on the fast rode another horse that dragged a travois carrying all the necessary things. The medicine man took a stake as tall as his shoulder and a heavy maul. Then he took the young man to a special place far away, knocked the stake into the ground clear to its tip and notched it. He took wet rawhide, wrapped it several times around the stake, and tied it with sinew. Then he took his knife and pierced the young man's chest very deep. He had let the wet rawhide dry so it was pointed and stiff like a pencil. When he pierced him, he put the rawhide through and pulled it way out and tied it with wet sinew so it would not come out. He said, "This will keep you here." Blood was streaming down. He chewed some medicine and put it on the cut to stop the flow. Then he left him.

When the medicine man came back to camp, he stopped on a hill and looked back. The medicine man hurt—never before had he experienced a situation like this and so he was heavyhearted. He stood there watching the young man until the sun set. He did that for two purposes: to see how the young man was reacting to the situation; and he wanted the rawhide that was soaked and limber to dry up, and the wet sinew that was tied on the ends to dry up.

When the sun set, the medicine man walked his horse home. At the evening meal, he told his wife and two sons, "Go ahead and eat. I feel very deeply for the young man I took out there. He is in constant pain and he will be there for three days and three nights. I am wondering how he will fare. So, my family, go ahead and eat. My concern is for him and I will fast along with him. I will smoke my Pipe and stay awake. I won't even lie down; I will sit in a chair and wait for daybreak to get here to help him in his prayer."

He was sitting there, hour upon hour, and toward daybreak, the Lakota people have a word, *ehake eyokpaza*, which means the last dark portion of the night before the first light of dawn. About that time the medicine man heard something heavy hit the ground. He thought that it was a neck yoke—the front piece of a wagon, and then it sounded as if someone slammed it against the outside wall. He got up and woke his two sons and told them, "Get up, there is something heavy that hit the back wall. Let us go out and check." They carried a lantern and found the young man on the ground outside the rear of the house. The pierced thong was still intact, as was the rawhide length attached to the stake. The long and heavy piece of timber that the medicine man had knocked into the earth that he was tied to had been pulled out of the ground and was lying there. The young man was unconscious.

They took a knife and cut his breast where the piercing was done. They cut the rawhide away, carried him inside, and placed him on a bed. They wet his face, fanned him, and he came to. He looked about. He did not know where he was. The medicine man told him, "They (the spirits) brought you back."

The young man said he was standing there, really tired, and he wanted to sit down. When he sat down the area changed to white, to red, to green, to yellow, and then it changed to darkness; that is all he knew.

In the evening of the same day, they went into a Pipe ceremony to find out why the young man had tried and failed for four consecutive summers. The spirits told the medicine man that the young man left out a portion of his sacred dream, and he should have told all of it.

When you pray to the Great Spirit, every word that you say must be meaningful. Sacred dreams are also that way. If you omit a portion of it, then it is nothing. When I had my sacred vision of getting two handfuls of hot coals in my hands, I knew it was dangerous. I knew it could cause me to lose my hands; I knew there could be hurt and pain. Common sense told me that I could be crippled for life. But if a person believes in and accepts a vision, it will be fulfilled.

When a person wants to go on a fast, the preparation has to be clear, precise, and true in form. Preparation is most important; it has to be done. Some will say that you can prepare one day and go on a fast the next. This is bullshit—it is these kinds of things that false medicine men tell people, which carry an absolutely false message.

There are many fakers across this land of ours, as well as the ministers on TV we hear so much about. You will not find a medicine man in a crowd; you will not find him in a pow-wow or a great gathering unless he is invited there.[13] A fake medicine man attending a great pow-wow will say he was invited there. These guys just give me a pain in the neck, and I know many of them. I could mention names, but I won't. And in not doing so, Wakan Tanka loves me all the more.

So, I see the difference in our world today and how different the people lived in the old Indian world many years ago. No wonder the Great Spirit loves the Lakota people—they did it right, they did it straight, they prayed in the Lakota language.

"*Tunkasila, Wakan Tanka, onsimilaye ikca wicasa onsia-makaagic. Mi takuye yoti wakinyan. Ikca wicasa ta cannunpa yuha. Hoye ciciye.*" This is the way we should pray.

WITHIN THE UNSEEN REALM
By Peter V. Catches (Zintkala Oyate)

I have come here for the past two years. This is my third fast with my Pipe. It is in the middle of the night of the third day. I have seen two sunrises and two sunsets, my inner self crying painful tears. This is the Spotted Eagle Way.

My father came here, as did his father before him; generation after generation the line continued as that of the first thought. This is the Pipe Way. You find peace in your heart and there is also fear. Its genesis is the sacred hoop, which has no beginning and no end.

I look skyward, and see the twinkling stars. I hear a rumbling and I know it is within me. I am hungry. I recall earlier in the hot day how thirsty I was, how my thoughts were hard to concentrate on prayer because of that physical thirst.

It is these physical barriers that haunt me now in the cold of the night. I clasp my Pipe harder and pray harder. It is my devotion, my personal path, and not like those of others before or after me. I know I am not alone in this unique prayer of fasting. I have become part of a universal creation, and know only that my spirit is growing. I know I have become a spiritual explorer to gain knowledge of peaceful acceptance of life, of being a part of it, and knowing that it is sacred.

Hanbleceya (Pipefast).

Memories in turn are another form of my mental and emotional growth. Except that I now look toward my future from this present place, always with hope and knowing that the Great Mystery is here with me now, encouraging my love of others and that I am special. I turn slowly in a clockwise motion until I face the west and sit down slowly, cross-legged, and tap into the umbilical cord of the Earth, my Mother. My physical presence is drained away, immediately replaced by a life energy with an awesome riveting beat, yet mildly flowing. I realize then that I have achieved another level in my spiritual journey.

"Wakan Tanka, Tunkasila, I pray to you as I stand up and turn to face the place where the dawn's light hides the stars and the morning star twinkles its last message to my heart. This heart of mine will always remain a doorway to that enlightened message. Great Mystery, your mysterious movement ignites a fire of love not ever wanting in my soul."

I hear the shrill of an eagle far away; it is getting closer. Then I feel that I am lying down. The sun is hot. I slowly sit up with my Pipe; I am somewhat bewildered. Then I remember, and I look around me and see the green, red, yellow, and gray tobacco tie flags, the tobacco tie fence, and the altar. Everything is as it should be.

I see that I must have slept most of the bright day. I stand up to see the medicine man and his helpers coming slowly. Upon arrival, he smudges the area with sweetgrass. Oblivious to me, he prays and then sings a song. The medicine man is followed by the one who carries the buffalo skull altar. No words are said; everyone is quiet.

»»→ • ←««

159

The fire at the *initi* has been burning throughout the time that I was fasting with my Pipe. The medicine man motions for me to go into the initi and sit in the back, opposite the door. He sits down to the right of the door opening and one of his helpers sits opposite him. Seven Tunkan are brought in one at a time, and then the living water is brought in and he prays with it and motions for the door to close. How I remember the eighth Tunka. I remember the day I came upon the stone and as clear memories held me, I had a peculiar fear—of the unknown in my quest, of loving the Great Mystery. I touched every little indentation in the stone, slowly and carefully picked this rock that I will know forever, and felt it to ask if it would help me someday. In my heart, I knew this was the humble way in which one should ask to be a part of the love and the key to its design.

I remember the other fasts. Now I more clearly see through the clouds of the darkened sky. I remember the eighth Tunka to help me come back anew. The first seven cleaned me and helped me here, that I might recognize the road and step slowly without fear in this path of virtue so lovingly handed down from our ancestors, guided by the Goddess of Harmony, that no thought can grasp Her beauty. Now I feel revived to live some more.

In the times I have come here, I have been shown that I am loved by an incomprehensible force which gave me this gift of love. The door is opened; the medicine man's helper takes sage and wipes my forehead, hands, and feet. The medicine man prays with a bowl of water and cherry juice to give to me to break my fast; it is bitterly wonderful. I am happy. The door closes. We sing together. Another door has opened, and we leave. Mitakuye oyasin.

Wiwangyang Wacipi (Sundance)

There is a proper way to go through with the ritual of a Sundance,[14] which takes place in the month of July. There are many versions, especially, shall we say, up-to-date versions. I think that early writers put too much "butter" on the thing. Young people today get the notion that a Sundance has to include torture and suffering as it was depicted years ago. A Sundance does not always entail the piercing of the flesh. A Sundancer can dance four full days without getting pierced and still be able to achieve his goals.

This ritual is very powerful when people do not abuse it. I use the word "abuse," because young bucks today have a tendency to abuse the sacred rituals given to us. A person can abuse the sweat lodge by making it too hot. The Sundance has also been abused. I have never seen Sundancers hung on the pole, but I have heard that in some places the dancers were hung in mid-air alongside the Sundance Tree. The Tree is sacred; we only put flags or offerings on the Tree.

When we go to a Sundance, we take in the whole picture. You see the crowd; there is always a big crowd. We have planned for the Sundance to take care of all the people's needs throughout the ceremony. At one side off at a distance is the kitchen where food is prepared for the elderly, the sick,

Petaga Yuha Mani praying during Sundance ceremony.

babies, young people, those who require food at the Sundance. Near the kitchen area is the water that the spectators may drink, because children, old people, and sickly people need water. We build shaded camping areas and outhouses that will accommodate the people who go there and camp. Then in the immediate area under the arbor where the crowd will gather, you have sick people sitting here and there. To the south of the arbor, where the white flags are, the drummers and singers are seated.

The Sundance Tree represents many things. First of all, it is a cane to lean on, to grow with, to hang on to. If it is a very hot day, you can sit in the shade of the Sundance Tree. I have seen this done very often. The Sundance Tree is commonly called the Tree of Life, because it gives life. It corrects our health problems, gives us a new lease on life. So, to dance the Sundance properly, one need not pierce the dancer's flesh. Dancing for four days, abstaining from food and drink is suffering enough. Four days of abstinence are enough to purge the impurities that have come into our lives.

On "Tree Day," the day we put the tree up, the scouts go out in search of the Sundance Tree. (They do not have to be scouts nowadays because we do not really live in the realm of the old world and the old Indian ways. But we call them scouts anyway.) The Sundance Tree could be several miles away. Everyone—the campers, the dancers, anyone present at the time—is privileged to go along, so a stream of cars goes to where the Sundance Tree is. The medicine man clears a place beneath the Sundance Tree, scatters some sage, and lets his Pipe rest there.

On occasion, the medicine man will talk to the crowd, explaining what is being done, because many of the people who have come to a Sundance for the first time will not understand. Four young girls are selected, dressed with deerskin and eagle feathers, who stand in readiness to perform the tree chopping ceremony. After the medicine man talks a bit about what is going to happen and its meaning, he fills his Pipe.

I will now focus on how I usually conduct a Sundance. Our presence there and all of the work involved in the Sundance, whether we pray or not, indicates that we are part of the Sundance prayer. I cannot tell all that goes through the mind of a Sundancer, because all are individual. I cannot tell you everything that goes on, because you have to be there to see and hear what takes place at a Sundance. What I am telling you here is what we do at our Sundance (on Pine Ridge) at Pte Woku (Feeding the Buffalo), an old residence of ours. Pte Woku is a nice location; our children grew up there. It is like a mesa (table) with lots of camping area, but it is a dry camp. We need a well there because we have the Sundance annually, and we have to haul our water. At Rosebud and elsewhere, they do it differently and they would talk about it differently.

When I start filling my Pipe for the four days of the Sundance, the drummer will be singing the Pipe-filling song, invoking the Four Directions, and their God-given power, so that the people shall live, that the coming generations will grow up and be plentiful, and that health and goodness will be among the people, and to take care of the elderly, and whatever our cares are at the time. In war years, such as World War II, the Korean conflict, and Vietnam, we audibly say prayers for the soldier boys. We never forget the sick who are in the hospital, those in prison, and relatives who are not with us now who have gone beyond the great divide. A red cloth flag with a tobacco pouch is tied to the tree, and red paint is smeared at the base of the tree. All these signify the intentions of people. All are in union at that moment beneath the Sundance Tree.

When the Pipe filling is done, we go into the Four Directions song, using the drum. My older son stands on one side of me, my youngest son stands on the other side, and we begin singing the songs to the Four Directions, to the heavens above, to the earth below. When this is done a medicine man directs the young maidens who are to chop the tree to give it one blow. He has instructed them how to do it, and he has told them why they were selected, that it is an honorable place and an honorable occasion, just like giving a person a name. He tells them that fifty years hence, when they have grown up to be old ladies with children and grandchildren, each one should be able to tell her children and grandchildren that at one time in her life she had the honor of giving the one chop of the hatchet to the sacred tree.

Each of the four girls takes a position in the one of the four directions beneath the Sundance Tree that is going to be cut down. According to instructions by the medicine man, the one to the west brings the hatchet and hits the tree at the base, at which time the crowd hollers what we call an akisa (called a war whoop by white people). The akisa invokes a blessing upon those who use their voices in the whoop. Next in the line is the girl to the north, followed by the one to the east, and last but not least, the one to the south.

The prayer at one place goes something like this: "Great Spirit, you have planted with your hand this tree at this particular place. The people have come from the center of the hoop and selected this tree that you planted here. They decorated it with a red flag and painted it red, signifying the race of people that you, the Divine Being, created. And in your inspiration, the people have at this time brought four maidens, very innocent in life, to give the first chop with the hatchet in the Four Directions, directions that you made sacred and holy, that henceforth where this Tree goes will be a holy and sacred place."

Next, a few people will use axes to start chopping down the Tree. The Tree is guided to fall in a particular direction, and the people stand on that side. Some use long branches, sticks, and poles to catch the falling Tree. When the Tree falls, it should not touch the ground. Women always have a place in our sacred ceremonies. If feasible, some will lay their shawls and blankets on the ground where the Tree will fall to prevent its branches and leaves from touching the earth. The Great Spirit planted this Tree here, and He let it grow to this height and size. The people came from within the sacred hoop to claim it, take it from this place where it was planted to the center of their hoop to replant it to become the Sundance Tree. Of course, because we are human and because the weather is all around us, some of the branches may touch the ground. These branches will be cut. Some do it right there, but in our case we just mark the branches and cut them when we take it back to the center of the sacred hoop.

A volunteer moves the Tree in a pickup; young men standing in the box or riding on the hood hold onto it so that it does not fall off. One year we even carried it on top of a van. We return to the Sundance ground in a procession with a filled Pipe taking the lead. When we arrive at a distance from the sacred hoop that we have agreed on, we stop the vehicles and unload the Tree there. The Sundancers and those who are able to carry the Tree on their shoulders take it to the entrance of the arbor.

On the way to the arbor, we stop four times. At the first stop, I pray and then we go on to the second stop. At the third stop, everyone yells the coyote howl as I have instructed them to do. I pray again. The fourth time we stop at the center of the sacred hoop, the center of the arbor where the Sundance will be held. In the center, a hole for the Sundance Tree has been dug in the ground. The women come forward with their shawls and blankets and lay them on the ground. The Sundance Tree is laid on the ground, and limbs that have touched the ground are trimmed off; the Tree is trimmed up to the fork. The fork of the Sundance Tree is a story in itself, which I will come to later.

I then perform a lengthy ceremony, asking the Great Spirit to bless the offerings of tobacco, water, *wasna* (ground dried meat with chokecherries), and buffalo blood. I offer the tobacco to the spirits that have passed on to the Great Divide since the last Sundance. Water is sprinkled in the hole and is likewise offered to the spirits who have left us—our relatives, close friends, and others. The wasna, too, is given to those spirits so that they can feed on it. In turn, these spirits will assist us in having a good Sundance. Each of the articles is offered to the four winds, praying all the while to Wakan Tanka to bless what is being offered.

When this portion of the ceremony is over, we select one person to take buffalo blood and wet the base of the Sundance Tree. When that is done, a cherry tree bundle, along with the offerings for the coming year, are placed in the crutch (fork) of the Tree and tied securely. The buffalo effigy, along with an effigy of a man, is tied toward the top of the Tree. Then the Sundancers who will pierce tie their ropes to the Tree.

When that portion of the ceremony is completed, we hoist the Sundance Tree to a standing position. When it stands in the hole, everybody, including children, grownups, and old people, give a yell rejoicing that a new life has begun, that we have entered into another phase of our life. When the Sundance Tree is tamped in solidly, the ropes that were loose are gathered together and tied at the base. The singers then launch into a song called Owanka Nasto. I would not attempt to try to translate the meaning of this song; it is too far beyond me.

During the singing of Owanka Nasto, everyone present dances—children, even sick people, and, especially in the old days, warriors. They dance at random, between the arbor area where the spectators will sit and the Sundance

Tree, which is in the center. It is a lengthy song. You have to make four complete rounds if you are a part of this dancing. You go around the inside of the arbor four times. When that is done, a rejoicing song of acceptance is sung because this is a happy occasion. You see smiles on people's faces because they know that they have witnessed the beginning of another year.

After the song of rejoicing, food is brought out and everyone sits in a circle. Lakota people often sit in a circle. (As a young boy I remember seeing old people sitting in a circle smoking the sacred Pipe. In those days, they carried a family Pipe, which they cherished and regarded as very sacred.) Young people volunteer to distribute food. We have Kool-Aid for the children, and coffee and tea; we have meat and soup; we have *wojapi* (berry pudding) and fry bread. It is a happy occasion. We enjoy the food of life, food that will be with us through the coming year.

The Sundancers are still with the people. This is the last food and drink of which they will partake. Right after the feasting is over, the dancers go off to one side into the sweat lodge. Perhaps that is the last time we will talk to them until after the Sundance, because they are kept in a secluded area. No one goes there except the person in charge, and myself. No one else goes near them. That is the true way of the Sundance. You do not allow people to come and talk to them. In order to have a good Sundance, you have to step on toes; you have to be a leader. You have to have your rules obeyed. Sometimes you even have to get angry. That is the role of a leader.

When the Sundancers are finished with the Purification Rite, they go into a teepee provided for them in the secluded area. But, some prefer to sleep under the arbor. A section of the arbor is reserved for them, fenced in with pine branches and pine limbs. They will sleep in the teepee or the reserved space in the arbor over the coming four days.

The Sundance is a hard prayer. For one thing, you abstain from food and water. The very first day, your throat is dry. On the second day, you have no spittle, your mouth is dry. The third day, your windpipe seems to crack up. On the fourth day, you do not know where you are, but you know someone or many people out there in the crowd are watching you, helping you. The dancing goes on no matter what kind of a day it is. In the years that I have Sundanced and directed Sundances, many times we danced in the rain and in the terrible summer heat of 110 degrees. Only a Sundancer knows how great the ordeal is.

I have seen Sundances at other places where Sundancers ate or drank in the evenings. To me, when Sundancers eat or drink during the four days they are abusing a sacred rite. If we do not respect ourselves, we should at least try to respect a sacred rite. If we cannot dance the Sundance four days and four nights, abstaining from food and water, we should have the respect to stay away from it. People who cannot abstain from food and water for four days but wish to participate can be a spectator, a drummer, a singer, a committeeman, or a worker who chops wood, keeps the fire going, among many other chores at a Sundance.

We have been having annual Sundances all on our own. For six years, just my family, my two boys, have somehow managed to put on a Sundance. But very recently, for two years now, we have had committees. We have people that we regard as Keepers of the Sacred Pipe and they, their families and their children, pledge to be a part of the Sundance sponsors. So, the going is lighter now. It is not as tough and hard as it was in previous years. Every year our crowd is getting bigger and bigger.

There are many things that go with the Sundance. Before this, I mentioned the crutch (fork) in the Sundance Tree. Sometimes you hear people who get involved with astronomy—the Tree itself is like a star map. If you look up at the sky at night, some clear night, especially in the summertime, you would see the cluster of stars called the Milky Way. If you study the Milky Way, it looks like the Sundance Tree. Maybe the first Indian who dreamed about the Sundance, who was chosen to understand and talk about the Sundance and its ways and its songs, knew that this Tree resembles the Milky Way.

Legend tells us that our next lives, after we leave this world, are like going through the Milky Way, or going up the Sundance Tree. There is an expanse of space, very much like we see in the heavens. The two stars that you see close by are perhaps millions of miles apart, and yet from our position, it seems to us that they nearly touch each other. So it goes in life. When our spirits walk the Spirit Trail, we come to this crutch or fork in the path. And according to legend, an Old Lady sits in the crutch and looks at us as we approach. If you

Petaga Yuha Mani praying at Sundance ceremony.

do not have *agito* (enlightenment), the Old Lady will point in the direction of the cut-off branch, and your spirit will follow that and go to an end where it falls off into space, into nowhere. When the Old Lady sees a person, a spirit, approaching and it is agito, she points to the long way, the remaining distance to the top of the Sundance Tree or to the top of the Milky Way, and the spirit can go on into that eternal reward, that everlasting bliss.

So the Sundance Rite, as given to us, means that we live in this world. But, if we do the Sundance Rite in a correct manner with our heart in it and dancing the four days, fasting from food and water, we will reach the very top of the Tree. The very top of the Sundance Tree will bring us everlasting life to be with the loved ones who have gone before us in order to be happy forever. This is one aspect of the Sundance that I love so much.

During an intermission of a Sundance where I was present, a person who is well known and very prominent—I will not mention his name—went to the sound system and gave a lengthy talk. In the course of his talk, he said, "Catches taught us many things, and when I look at the man Catches, I think that this Sundance arbor is his home. I think he lives here." My experiences in the many Sundances that I have conducted and was a part of show me that the Great Spirit is present in all the things that we do. I hope that some of you who read this book will understand a little about the Sundance at our place, at Pte Woku. And I hope that through this little talk of mine, the Great Spirit will love you and bless you and those whom you care for.

>>>—→ • ←—<<<

The Lone Sundancer

By Peter V. Catches (Zintkala Oyate)

I sing the songs of my grandfathers, who were medicine men in their respective clans of the Lakota oyate. I am in this Purification Rite that precedes what I am to do, to cleanse my spirit in order to approach the sacred ground—the circle underneath the Tree of Life.

It is dawn as I prepare myself inside the Inipi, the first rite of the people. I tell the Tunkan (the birth and the aged) of this dream, which has haunted me for what seems like an eternity. Now I am here to shed that pain and feel its entirety.

I have done the Hanbleceya (Pipefast) for four consecutive years, yet the vision persists to make me new, in a day that is yet to dawn. I have tried to avoid its essence many years, because of the shame brought upon us by a different people who believed differently.

Now, by the instructions of the medicine man, both of us chant. In the reality of the chant, we steam ourselves before we leave the sacredness of the Inipi. It is still dawn; I am taken by two helpers who sew seven *wanble gleska weyaka* (spotted eagle feathers) on my arms, with one in the middle of my back.

The drum to the south begins a rapid, nonuniform beat. We walk slowly from the west, outside the perimeter of the prayer sticks, slowly toward the red tobacco flags to stop and implore the formless Wakinyan (Thunder Beings), who are the West, to bless this day. We continue and stop at the North, with its two long red tobacco tie flags, to implore the

Tatanka Oyate (Buffalo Nation), and for them to hear our plea with this sacred Pipe. We continue and stop the third time, to implore the Wicasa Wan Kaiglaglag (Radiantly Golden Man), who gives us this sacred day. Then, we continue on to the east and stop for the last time at the two long yellow tobacco tie flags before we enter the sacred hoop of the Sundance Nation. Here we implore the Pahan San Oyate (Gray Swan Nation) to the south to bless this area of prayer in their divine flight.

The medicine man takes me inside the hoop. He walks in a sacred way inside its perimeter toward the two long gray tobacco tie flags and on to the two long green tobacco tie flags, where he fashions an altar of sage and the buffalo skull. There he slowly places my lone Pipe.

I turn to the right of the sacred Tree of Life to face the glorious dawn. The drums beat in unison. My thoughts look upon the east; I feel the chill of the morning air. I hear the hush of beauty in my soul. The song of the ancients is in the air; my essence vibrates with its rhythm and my spirit awakens to the words of the song.

> *Anpetu ki le wakan yelo.*
> *Tokahe ya taku wa yelo.*
> *Wanble gleska wan le ya*
> *kinyan u welo.*
> *Anpetu ki le wakan yelo.*
> *Tokahe ya taku wa yelo.*
> *Anukan san wan le ya*
> *kinyan u welo.*

>>>→ • ←<<<

This is a holy day.
I am the first relative of this day.
A spotted eagle is saying this
as he comes.
This day is holy.
I am related first to this day.
A bald eagle is saying this
as he comes flying.

The first rays of the sun break in the east and tears flow inside. I feel the awe of the moment.

It has been hours; my dancing is like breathing. My perspiration is like another skin, soothing and cooling me. It is then that the medicine man with another helper takes me by both arms and makes a wide clockwise circle in the hoop of the nation. I am slowly laid down under the Tree of Life with my head toward the altar. I close my eyes to feel a sharp pain above my heart and feel myself being lifted to my feet. "Wakan Tanka (Great Spirit), pity me," is the song that is sung.

The medicine man and his helper have left the sacred area. I am alone. My thoughts race back in time—the songs take me there. The four great virtues loom in front of me. I slowly make my selfless plea for wisdom on behalf of the entire community. This plea is made to the universal forces, which I understand to be superior to mankind. I have offered this flesh, for I understand that this is the one thing that is mine alone, mine alone to give. I sacrifice myself in this way. I realize that this area in my reality is the entire universe—the sacred Tree of Life has become Wakan Tanka (Great Spirit), my flesh is ignorance, and the skewers in my flesh are the rays of enlightenment that I receive from the Great Spirit.

By enacting my vision, I have offered my sacrifice, clarifying my willingness to accept an attitude of submission, my equality of obligation to those greater things that we know to be superior to ourselves. This obligation of equality I acquiesce to and invite the rest of the people to join in. This equality whose members possess equal respect for one another.

In doing this, I am symbolically submitting to the Sundance Nation in what I perceive to be the rightful location in the nest of creation, and providing the means for acquiring equality of respect and trust. I effortlessly push back the borders of my rightful community into a realm that is beyond simple description. I Sundance, with the forces, with the people, the Sundance Nation.

The sun is overhead at its zenith. I am lost no longer, yet the intensity is mystifying, for I feel no pain. And though I cry inside, I know that the vision is just beginning. I feel the power in my sacrifice and I am weary. I know there is a power inside of me, giving me what I need to go on, and I feel happiness to have come this far.

The sun is falling rapidly; the ancient songs are enhancing the sacred area of worship. Over toward the west the Thunder Beings loom as they approach forebodingly. Their shapeless forms rumble and their eyes are spears of searing light. I feel an uneasiness that makes me tremble.

They are coming low, stomping the earth. The people are afraid; I know what must be done.

I call for my sacred Pipe, and it is given to me. This is the haunting dream, the painful reality. I slowly lift my sacred Pipe toward the thunderhead, close my eyes, and whisper the sacred words from the Land of the Winds. The reality of my sacrifice bounds forth with my faith. It is an inspiration so deep, guided by a just belief, that upon opening my eyes the thunderhead is parted. And suddenly, in between the parted storm clouds flies the spotted eagle. It is over. The feathers sewn on my arms seem to come alive. Joy unfolds inside my soul; the feeling is of pure ecstasy. The feathers pull me upward and I dance to the rhythm. With outstretched arms and feathers whirling, I run backwards and feel myself break free.

This vision, this sacred dream completed, only reveals the Red Road of Life. The path of the Pipe religion of the Sundance Oyate is a connection between religion and philosophy, with the practice of good living. It is an inspirational foundation based upon an experiential religion. Everyone becomes a member, and above all, a holy being created by God.

Hunkapi (Making of a Relative)

The Making of a Relative is one of the Seven Sacred Rites given to the Lakota people. I will not go into full detail as to what it really means. But the beginning part of it is that on the anniversary of losing people we love who have left this world and gone into the Great Hereafter—children, grandchildren, brothers, and sisters—we commemorate the occasion and remember them with a feast. When we lose a member of our families, we seek solace and comfort. The way the Indian people do this is to make a relative of someone living to replace the one we lost. In this way, the only way to acquire the nearness of those we lost is to make a relation of someone who makes us think of them because of their appearance, disposition, character, or way of life. We tend to bring that person into our family group, to become one of us in the absence of the real one. In our culture, we think what that we do with the adopted one is the same we would do with the one we have lost.

According to this way of thinking and the way of life that Wakan Tanka gave to us, we have this sacred rite. We can make a relationship or a friendship with anyone, and as implied, we have to go through a ceremony. The way to do that is to go through a sweat lodge ceremony to prepare ourselves physically and spiritually with the one that we are to make a relative. In preparing for this ceremony, the women go to beading deerhide moccasins and dresses. There are many types of buckskin dresses with many designs on them. There are also headpieces, necklaces, the front wide pieces, and belts. Some of these will be given to people at the giveaway part of the ceremony.

When going into the ritual, a white cloth is stretched between two poles, denoting that the loved one has crossed over. The white connotes purity. We on each side will come together in purity, resembling this white cloth, in spirit and physically.

»»—→ • ←—««

There are certain songs for this occasion and a certain kind of drumbeat. A gourd with an ear of corn mounted on the handle, and another stick with horsetail hair hung at the end are shaken in time with the beat of the drum. The people are dancing along throughout, touching both parties during the time the gourd is shaking in time with the drum.

The dancers make a complete circle. The song is repeated four times: to the west, and they dance in that direction, to the north and they dance to that direction, to the east and they dance to that direction, and to the south, they in turn dance to that direction, making a complete circle.

The two who are united in relationship are touched with the horsetail hair. This requires a certain amount of skill because you have to be able to keep time with the gourd in your left hand. The spectators who watch these ceremonies see the sacredness. Even awkward, slow-moving, unlively people become lively and skillful dancers when handling the gourd and the ear of corn.

The medicine man who conducts the ceremony then gives water and food, praying with it and placing it there. The two becoming related must feed each other. One feeds the new relation, and the new relation feeds the one that fed him. This is unity, a coming together, in prayer, action, and song, in a physical way and in spirit. Blessed by the Great Spirit, becoming relatives by a sacred rite that begins at that moment, to last forever in this world and on into the next.

When this part of the ceremony is over, we go feast. There is much feasting, all provided by the person who makes a relation of someone. A large crowd is fed, and then there is a giveaway, bundles of articles accumulated over the past year. We like to talk about generosity. If you attend these ceremonies, you will see what generosity entails.

When you go to a restaurant and sit down to a good meal, an exceptionally good meal, you remember it and tell your friends, "That restaurant is a good one. They served me good food, and they made me comfortable. I felt at home." So, too, in this feasting at the Making of a Relative, there are many kinds of food. The amount of food is so plentiful that everyone is well fed, and parts of the food are taken home. We call it *wateca*, and it is like taking a part of the feast to those at home. There might be a sick person at home unable to attend the gathering; through wateca, they are able to partake of some of this feasting food, blessed on the occasion by the Great Spirit.

The Indian people look at food as the number one medicine, the first food that man lives on. We consider food to be medicine because we are sustained by it and we gain strength from it; because we are happy when we are well fed and glad to be alive. We then look at life from another perspective. We are thankful that we can go on with good food in us, making us strong and happy, and this food is carried home.

Many things are given away to visitors, so that when they go home, in the directions of the four cardinal points of the compass, they will say, "I received this at that Making of a Relative sacred rite ceremony. They gave much food away, they gave horses away, they gave money away." The tidings are taken home, and people who were not present will know that there are two people who became relatives on that occasion.

I experienced this Making of a Relative twice in my life. Once I was made a little brother to Silas Black Dog of Rosebud country. He is originally from Rosebud, but he married into the Lower Brulé tribe, where he lived and passed away. Over in the Rosebud country, at Spring Creek, I was adopted into the Paul Swift Hawk family, so I have relatives there as I speak. I have younger sisters, younger brothers, I have nieces, nephews, and grandchildren living in Spring Creek at this time. My brother Silas Black Dog passed away early in 1970 and my father Paul Swift Hawk passed away several years ago.

It is good to note that Wakan Tanka, in His goodness, takes care of His people. I do not know what a father is, and I really do not know what a mother is. When I was very young, I lost my father and mother. But, the Great Spirit saw to it that in the life of Paul Swift Hawk, he chose to make me his son. I became his oldest son, because their first-born passed away when the boy was in infancy. And if this boy were alive, my adopted father told me, he would have been exactly my age. A coincidence that I should mention is that my real father's first name is Paul, and my adopted father's first name is also Paul.

My relations in Spring Creek are much cherished and we love one another. I used to spend parts of every summer there. Just recently, I received an emergency message that the Pine Ridge police delivered to my trailer camp. A younger brother, Ben Swift Hawk, passed away at Spring Creek. My wife and I traveled to Rosebud country and attended the wake and funeral of my brother Ben at Spring Creek. At the funeral, I sang a song during the covering of the grave.

Afterward I dreamed about my little brother Ben. At first, I did not know it was him. I saw an Indian with long hair in regalia with an eagle feather tied to his head. The horse he was riding was restless, eager to go, high-spirited. When the warrior on this horse moved at a certain angle, I could see certain parts of his cheek; he was wearing war paint. Down in the canyon was a river, and among the trees I could see thirteen or fourteen buffalo. Some were lying down, others were standing in the river, drinking water, and still others were under the trees.

Over to the right, below a sloping hill, was a blanket of sage and brush. In the brush and the sage I could see three or four deer and a few antelope. In this scene a buffalo bull was bellowing and screaming. I looked his way and he was pawing the earth, pawing dust upon his back. Above the horizon I could see an eagle soaring. By that time the mount of the warrior had spun around; he was eager to run. And when the horse spun around, I saw the warrior fully in the face—it was my little brother Ben.

I called the Swift Hawk family members by phone and told them about this dream. Soon afterward, we made a hurried trip over there, and I told my sister, Sarah, the dream I had of my little brother. That gave solace and comfort to the family. The dream has quite a few meanings, but in general, it is wonderful and beautiful.

The old Lakota way of life is very precious to me. Relationships were very firm in the Indian world at that time.

Petaga Yuha Mani filling his sacred Pipe.

A common relationship is seen as medicine, as food, and its worth is beyond measure. The relationship entails everything. It entails love, like father-in-law love, mother-in-law love. Love is the main principle in Lakota family life.

Today we hear so much about family child abuse in the newspapers, on the radio, and so on. This type of abuse was unknown in the old Indian world. Relationships and relatives were held in very high esteem. When relatives such as cousins would see each other in the morning, they would shake hands, and then shake hands again if they see each other in the evening. They would go out of their way to do their relations favors. The need of a relation was considered to be one's own.

An example of the importance of relationship involves two cousins. One cousin was away for quite a while, close to two months. When he returned he was told that his cousin was very sick. So the first thing he did was saddle his horse to visit his cousin. When he found his cousin sick in bed, he went to him, shook his hand, and embraced him. There was deep sorrow in the cousin who went to see the sick man, but he did not want to break into crying. He wanted to show his cousin that he is firm and strong. This is the medicine way of the Lakota people.

Today, under the same circumstances, the one going to the sick person might shake the cousin's hand, embrace, and start crying. Crying, in a sense, weakens a sick person. In the past, everyone knew that. Through the ages, through generations of nature's teachings, people understood that when they see or go to see a sick person, they must be strong. They have one word to give to that one sick person: *blaheceya*. I do not know how to translate that word. But, in the Indian world, they say that is the beginning of a doctoring.

Even when getting a cup of water to give to a sick person, we would say these words: *"le yatkan yo a nicisni ktalo"* ("Drink this water and you will get well"). Every word, every action in the Lakota world was part of helping one another, reaching out to help. Even common words were said as words of encouragement. These words had strength, gave strength and hope.

So the cousin visited the sick cousin and they talked about old times. Upon leaving his sick relation that evening, he said, "I am going home now, but I will come again tomorrow. But, tahansi, get well. We will join the Buffalo Bill Wild West Show in the spring, and we will travel to many cities, maybe cross the ocean together. We will see some sights, so get well. When I get home, I will tell my sisters and my cousins to make you two pairs of beaded moccasins, and two pairs of beaded moccasins for me. I will see to it that I get your Indian regalia completed, and mine also. By the time the Buffalo Bill Wild West Show begins, we should be joined up with the outfit."

This was in the fall. So through the winter months the sick cousin had his sights set on this Buffalo Bill's Wild West Show, and he worked very hard to get well. And it is told that he did get well, and that both cousins spent six months with the show and then returned home.

The Seven Sacred Rites

The Lakota have many rites and ceremonies, but there are seven major sacred rites given to the Lakota by White Buffalo Calf Woman. As mentioned previously, the seven are the Purification Rite (Inipi), Sundance (Wiwangyang Wacipi), Pipefast (Hanbleceya), Making of a Relative (Hunkapi), Throwing of the Sacred Ball, Coming of Age (also known as Making of the Buffalo Woman), and Keeping and Releasing of the Spirit. Four of the seven have been discussed above, and the remaining three are briefly described below.

The Throwing of the Sacred Ball ceremony is carried out when the Lakota nation's survival is at stake. This ceremony is not being held or directed by a medicine man at the present time, but may be reintroduced if the need arises in the future.

The Coming of Age, or Making of the Buffalo Woman, is a rite solely for young women who have reached puberty. Medicine women carry out this long ceremony. Because Lakota society is matriarchal, there is a sacred ceremony dedicated exclusively to women. (There is no comparable ceremony for men.)

Finally, the Keeping and Releasing of the Spirit ceremony is aimed at restoring communal unity, that is, to heal the shattered unity of families. For this ceremony, the medicine man spends time with members of the family and advises them on what they should do heal the unity over a one-year period. After the year has ended, certain rituals are conducted.

Pete Catches tending the sacred fire.

Five *(Zaptan)*
BEGINNINGS
& ENDINGS

Oceti Wakan

THE DEVASTATION

The greatest evils of our time are alcohol and drug abuse. In the course of a little more than six weeks, my wife and I attended seven wakes and funerals. Most were alcohol-related deaths. Even babies die from alcohol—they get run over or other things happen to them as a result of adults using alcohol. One baby that died through alcohol-related causes was from my big brother's family line. The next baby that died was from my blind sister's family line.

One of the seven funerals was in the Rosebud country. I mentioned earlier that Rosebud country is where I was adopted into a family in 1968. The family's name is Swift Hawk. I got an emergency call that one of the family members passed away, so my wife, my son, and I went to Rosebud. That death was also alcohol related—a man in his sixties was beaten to death.

I do not like to see people crying. I want to see happiness in people. You see children laughing and playing, and it does your heart good. That is the way life should be. I had to go to all these wakes and funerals because the deceased are a part of our people. We shed tears nearly every day because of alcohol, drugs, AIDS, and other things that trouble our people, that cause orphans, that cause loved ones to go away into the next world.

We have a tribal council, a legislative body that oversees the tribe. I doubt that there is a councilman big enough to attack the problem of alcohol. At another reservation, the tribal council recently went to war against alcohol. I admire the people who initiated this. Support for the war against alcohol was also given by the tribal law and order committee, policemen, judges, and other personnel involved in working for the tribe. If people living on that reservation are convicted on an alcohol-related charge, including drunk driving, they are given a chance to rehabilitate by going to treatment voluntarily. They can return to their jobs when they finish their treatment. But if they do not accept treatment, they lose their jobs and are usually imprisoned.

I believe that the Pine Ridge Reservation needs the type of leadership you see in the Dads Against Drunk Driving (DADD) organization. They walk the highways in protest against the things that are going wrong here. I admire the people in DADD and I work with them. They too, are my relatives. Another organization is Mothers Against Drunk Driving (MADD), and still another is SADD (Students Against Drunk Driving). We made the public aware of these organizations. The protests and marches we organized were broadcast by the KILI radio station, the

Lakota Times, and the *Rapid City Journal.* These organizations are now known throughout the United States, Canada, and elsewhere.

The Oglala Sioux tribal council on several occasions wanted to legalize alcohol on the reservation. The issue went to a referendum, and the people turned it down. It does not matter who the person is, or what profession or career a person has, if he has a bottle of alcohol in one hand, I do not look at him as a man. In order to do good, dependable work, a man must do away with the bottle and live in sobriety for people to see. A sober person does not have to advertise. He can live sober and people will notice. This is where trust begins and will remain.

I am not saying sobriety is easy. Sobriety is hard to live when all around you people are drinking. But sobriety to me is the one thing that the so-called Jesus Christ would love to see. Tunkasila, Wakan Tanka, loves a person who does not use alcohol, because alcohol is the ruin of our people. Alcohol would not be part of the world if we had strong leaders such as Crazy Horse and Sitting Bull. These men were true leaders, and they loved their people. There is no one like them now.

When the white man came west, he brought the evil along with him. He brought rotgut whiskey, syphilis, gonorrhea, and now AIDS. If we were left alone to live as we were before the advance of the white man, we would still be able to live in a clean and pure fashion, take care of our ourselves, teach our children respectability, to respect the elders, the sick, to help one another, to live in harmony. This is how Wakan Tanka made us.

>>>➤ • ←《《《

How can we be happy with all the tears? Even people who will die natural deaths are bothered with alcohol. People who do not drink at all are bothered by friends and relatives for money, for things to hock, you name it. They knock at your door at all hours of the day and night. They stop you in the street and ask you for a quarter. It is good to help once in a while. But, many of the sober people are like myself. Sometimes I go without because I do not have it. Sometimes my car runs near empty, and here are people asking for money to buy alcohol.

I hear many people saying we are having these problems because some do not do the Sundance right, they do not do the sweat lodge right, and they do not do the Pipefast right. And suffering falls upon the people. In the many Sundances throughout the reservation, I see dancers who partake of food and water in the evening, and that is all wrong. We should try to do at least a portion of the Sundance the authentic way, the way it was originally done. Our forefathers practiced the real Sundance, the real Pipefast, and the real sweat lodge ceremony. So, why could we not continue with the traditions sacred to our people and to Wakan Tanka? Why did He give us these Seven Sacred Rites? In doing the ceremonies the traditional ways we can communicate with Him, and He will do for us what we ask.

I used to drink, and I used to go to jail. But, I quit all on my own with Wakan Tanka's help. I quit not because I was sick of it with cirrhosis. I quit not because I went to AA (Alcoholics Anonymous) meetings or to treatment. In turn, I pledged that all the remainder of my life would be in sobriety. That is a hard commitment to make.

I used to listen to people who said, "I am going to quit for forty days." These are people who go to church. Through Lent (forty days prior to Easter), they abstain from some things that they like. Some abstain from smoking, some from alcohol; some say they are going to cut down on their food consumption.

One day I got up with a hangover. I had a splitting headache. Out of habit, I began looking for some beer. I would usually find it outside somewhere, because I had been sitting outside and drinking and would leave some there. Or I would look in the refrigerator over in the next house. I went through the whole bit and could not find anything. So, I came back and sat on my bed. At the head of my bed was an apple box. On the box stood a lamp and "the makings," as we call it—Bull Durham, cigarette paper, and matches. And sitting there thinking about it, I looked up and there in plain sight on the table stood a whole pint of wine. Not even the seal was broken.

I had mixed feelings. I was glad, but yet when I looked at that wine, a thought came to me. I thought of Wakan Tanka, why he made me. A thought came to me: if I lived in the old Indian world, I would have been a warrior. Most certainly, I would have been a warrior, and a warrior fights enemies. So looking at that wine, I said, "Wakan Tanka, make me a warrior." I got up and went over to that bottle of wine, hit it on the bottom three or four times, broke the seal, and unscrewed the cap. And I said this: "Wakan Tanka made me a warrior, and you are the enemy of the people. This moment you and I clash in a struggle, in a fight—I as a warrior, you as an enemy of me and the Lakota people." I opened the door, stepped outside on the porch, and I turned that bottle upside down.

Part of me was saying, "Turn it back over, save a mouthful," that sort of thing. But, I held on to the idea that I was a warrior and engaged in a struggle. I emptied the whole bottle, and held it in my hand: "Today I conquered you and I scalped you." Then I threw that bottle as far as I could, and I said, "A warrior is honored by the scalps that he acquires. But I do not even want your scalp. I will throw that away, too." Then I threw the cap away. And to this day, I have not swallowed a drop of any kind of alcoholic beverage.

Alcoholism is an example of what life is about today. When we partake of alcohol, we live in a sort of imitation happiness. We do not think right. Everything that we do is false. The happiness we seem to enjoy is false. The laughter is there, but it is false. The real world is sobriety. It is a hard world with many problems. But being sober and honest, living good, is the life that Wakan Tanka loves. This is the life that He wants us to live.

When parents drink, it makes children nervous, causes them to lose sleep and miss school. Sometimes they go to school without having breakfast. It takes food out of the mouths of children, because parents spend food money on alcohol. This is why I say that alcohol is the greatest evil of our time.

THE HEALING

Because of alcohol, drugs, and other problems, I had an idea years of ago of establishing a spiritual encampment, Oceti Wakan (Sacred Fireplace). At Oceti Wakan, we will teach in our Lakota language and use the Pipe and the sacred ceremonies that were given to us by the Great Spirit to overcome the evils of our time.

As a medicine man, I want to be instrumental in doing things with the sacred Pipe, imploring the Great Spirit for the things that mankind cannot do. In trying to explain Oceti Wakan, I will say it this way. When the Great Spirit, Wakan Tanka, created the world and the many things that comprise this creation, He made people in the many colors that He liked. Wakan Tanka likes color. He made the black people, the white people, the yellow people, and the red people. The red people are the Eskimos, the Canadian Indians, and the Native Americans of the fifty states and down through Mexico and South America.

To each of these different peoples, He gave language, traditions, customs and culture, each different from the other, because His love is there. To these many different colored peoples that He made, He gave to each a way to worship. He gave the white people Jesus Christ; to others, He gave Buddha, to others a different One. And in that way, He gave the red people a way of life, a culture, a language, heritage, and tradition. He gave the red people a language to pray to Him, a culture completely different from that of the others. It is through this system of prayer and language, a way of life, that we can address whatever problems may assail us in this life on earth.

He gave the sacred Pipe to pray with to the Lakota people. I believe most sincerely that the Lakota can stop this alcohol and drug abuse through the use of the sacred Pipe in the proper way, and through the language, the culture, the traditions, as they were given to us many centuries before the white men arrived on these shores.

Oceti Wakan will be unique. It will be a place of worship. One of the four things that Lakota people use in praying to the Great Spirit is fire. As I have said, Oceti Wakan means Sacred Fireplace, one of the places we pray from. A sacred fireplace is the fire pit at the head of the sweat lodge, and where the fire is built during a Sundance. The sweat lodge will be conducted year round. I am old now, and I cannot go to a sweat lodge in the wintertime when it is cold. But, the winter sweat lodge will be built inside a ceremonial house with a dirt floor, and the summer sweat lodge will be out in the open. And if it should rain during the summertime, we can go in that house and still conduct our sweat lodge. Maybe we will have a sweat lodge ceremony every morning or every evening. This is what we call Indian time, or when events do not have to be at a particular time. I remember one day we had several sweat lodge ceremonies—one at daybreak and another at about ten o'clock, and then another about two or two-thirty, and one before the sun set. We had four sweat lodge ceremonies in one day. Oceti Wakan would be something like this, a cleansing place. The sweat lodge ceremony is really a purifying ceremony—it cleanses the spirit and the body, the physical being.

We are in this life just once, and the days we live will never come back again. So from this aspect, from this vision, I know Oceti Wakan, if it ever materializes, will do good for our people. I have not much more in life to go, so while I am able, I wish to put everything that I can into it. My heart is in it; my mind is in it, my body is in it, my spirit is in it. And if it is the will of the Great Spirit, it shall come to pass. If Oceti Wakan does not ever get off the ground, then I know it is not the time. Then I would know that the Great Spirit has a time for such an endeavor, and maybe somebody more worthy than I am. If I am unworthy, I will know that this thing will not come to pass.

This is the way I want to teach. This is the way I want to instill in minds and hearts a faith and trust so strong in the Great Spirit that they can be cured of any terrible disease such as alcohol and drugs. With this faith and trust in the Great Spirit, anyone can be cured, because that is His word. And if we live in that way, we will know we are part of His creation, that we are part of this growing Earth. From a sad state of alcoholism, we can become whole again, become rich in spirit, become loved by the Great Spirit, because we are a part of His creation.

My philosophy goes something like this. There is in this creation Wakan Tanka, and He created man. He instilled into every human being a source of power, a gift, and with that, he can overcome any amount of problems in his whole lifespan. But many people let the gift lay dor-

Okawinga Win (Amelia Emily Ribsman Catches), 1991.

mant, unused. If we only reach out and look for the source of that extra strength, we can overcome anything. If we can overcome one problem, we can overcome any other problem that assails us. In this way, we will prove to ourselves and to our God, our Wakan Tanka, that His work on earth is growing in His love.

There are beautiful hills and pines at Pte Woku. There are deep canyons; they are all beautiful. God's hand is there. I want to put my hand next to His and implore Him through these sacred rites, in my own language, to cure our people from the diseases of alcohol and drugs, and live a life that comes from Him, a life in the light of truth, in the light of love and the beauty of being alive and being good. This is just the beginning of Oceti Wakan.

Land of the Winds

By Peter V. Catches (Zintkala Oyate)

The drums beat in rhythm and guttural voices chant in unison in an ancient tongue. Sorrow is in the surrounding atmosphere; the loss of a precious soul is in the chant. "The time is right; my life's prayer is done," he said in the days before his journey of eternal life. His last words as dawn broke were, "The answer to my prayer is complete and once more is one. I see in the darkest hour before the dawn, the icon of the people, the icon of the Spirit Trail, in the star clusters of heaven's light. There is a new light shining in my soul, which encompasses the nature of my being. Great

>>>→ • ←<<<

Spirit, Grandfather, with this sacred Pipe I send my spirit, for with my relatives I will live again. Grandfather, help me, pity me, I am having a hard time," were his last words as dawn broke.

It is December 3, 1993. At 3:49 in the morning, this holy man, Petaga Yuha Mani, was taken back by the Great Spirit (Wakan Tanka). This renowned medicine man of the Teton Lakota had been an integral part in bringing the Sundance ceremony out in the open. Surely, he shall be missed. There is no confusion among the people of the Lakota oyate about who this man is. Petaga Yuha Mani was the kind of man who showed the unconquerable force of love, and in so doing, he brought generations together on the plateau of understanding. He had said that we cannot force peace, nor can we buy peace; only through the love of humanity can we achieve peace.

Our faith in the motion of creation, with its inspiration of just beliefs, leads us directly to the sacred truth—that we are all brothers and sisters and that we have a collective inheritance in the love of the Great Spirit. In the heat of misunderstanding, ridicule, and reproach, he took that step in bringing the Pipe religion to the surface for the world to see. He stood forth in developing harmonious relations with all people.

In September 1990, Petaga Yuha Mani traveled to Russia and did a tree planting ceremony with children. These are his words: "It was cold and windy; I filled my Pipe. I did the ceremony in my own language, but of course, they didn't know the Dakota language. Then in English I told the interpreter what I had said. These little children standing here, I want them to go first, to get a handful of dirt and throw it around the tree. He translated what I said to the children and they all moved forward. I continued by telling them that they and Russia itself, will grow to see peace, and to learn from one another. 'This tree is young, like you children, and it will grow as you children grow.'"

Petaga Yuha Mani was the kind of man who experienced insult and emotional injury, yet he displayed an irrepressible courage with an unshakable faith in his belief in the sacred Pipe. He was a man dedicated to peace and understanding. His vision, his sacred dream, brought to him and instilled in him the key. As he would say, "I am in a natural place, where the soul constantly expands in the presence of beauty." He exalted his love of friendships and shared his knowledge wherever and whenever possible. His personal shortcomings did not stop him from hoping to see an illuminated world, filled with love, peace, true happiness, and the glowing grace of the Great Spirit.

My father's wish was to not be embalmed, and to have his body laid to rest about four hundred yards east of the Pte Woku Sundance area. I recall some of his words at my mother's funeral just three and a half months prior. He had said that in the past, the Lakota oyate had their main burial grounds in the sacred Black Hills. There a place had been reserved for chiefs, medicine men, and great warriors, and since the consciousness of America is now more understanding of religious freedom, we should by all means establish such a place again.

He said once before that death is not the end, but rather a beginning in the truest form. This, he said, would be the case for men, women, children, and elderly persons who had passed on to the Great Hereafter, the Happy Hunting Grounds, or Heaven. In our language, we say, "Tate Makoca," which means "Land of the Winds." We understand that we should honor and respect the life of the departed one, that we should acknowledge and accept that individual's principles even though we may not know the extent of them. Last of all, we must obey the final wishes of the departed and be happy for them, for they have gone to a place where they have gained the reality, love, and grace of the Great Spirit.

I recall that before my mother's funeral, my father came to me and said that we should not cry , and those same words echoed in my mind on the day of his funeral. How could I not cry when I loved him so much? I cannot escape the magnitude of my sorrow. Seeing the grief of the many people whom he helped and affected throughout his life touched me deeply, and I could not take it anymore. I broke down and cried; I could no longer contain my sorrow, and so I broke that wish. Yet in retrospect, I believe that it was meant to be that way. We must understand human nature as our Pipe religion offers it. We have to experience the various qualities of our lives in order to fully participate in, understand, and accept life as it is.

On December 7, 1993, the morning of my father's burial, while everything was being prepared, my wife, sisters, brothers, and close relatives and friends agreed that we should have the giveaway and feeding for the people first. In December, before the solstice (December 21) when winter begins, the days were very short. Our concern was with the light of day available to us.

On December 4 and 5, we had a ground blizzard, also known as a whiteout. The day we brought his body home, the sun was out, the air was warm, and the sky was blue. The manner in which he had wanted his burial conducted necessitated a one-night wake, with the burial the following afternoon. His casket was sealed, and so we had hung his portrait above his casket. He laid in my mother's house at Mission Flat, a part of the Calico community, located three miles northwest on Highway 18 from the town of Pine Ridge.

Never to my knowledge had a circumstance such as this ever occurred before. Usually the departed were buried, and then the people were fed, and a giveaway would occur a year later. As I should have said before, close relatives had donated the cow for beef to make stews and soups for the feed. Other relatives and friends brought flowers, cards, and food in paying him their last respects. A close relative from Manderson was accompanied by a friend who brought his team of horses and wagon for Petaga Yuha Mani's last bodily trip.

People came from throughout Lakota country, parts of Canada, and the United States. In our own community where everyone is related, most of us felt that the Great Spirit had let my father live until now. Two years ago, he was given ten days to live, and released from the hospital. I was in Florida at the time, yet relatives were able to reach me to tell me to return because he was asking for me. I returned home to learn he was staying at one of my sister's friend's homes in the Black Hills. Several of his acquaintances told me at that time that he would like to die in the sacred Black Hills.

I thought about that day, more than two years ago, when I was told a Sundance was about to commence west of the town of Custer in the Black Hills. I went to that place, and found him in a square-walled tent. As I entered the tent, there was a soft mattress with bedding and other blankets and quilts. To the immediate left of the entrance, there were many types of food and liquids for him to drink. He was lying on the bed made for him. He looked up and smiled, and that mutual love of father and son that no words can express or explain was in the air. I knelt down before him, we embraced, and to this day, I remember my prayer as I had said it then.

"My friends toward the West, you have said, look this way. You are the Great Thunder Beings who gather at the setting sun's horizon. You have made me see. My friends toward the North, I look that way, to see the Buffalo Nation, beautifully coming in a holy way. You have made me see. My friends toward the East, my mind goes there, to see the Elk Nation, as They do the holy dance in the glorious morning. You have made me see. My friends toward the South, where the warm winds come, I see the Gray Swan Nation, coming this way in their divine flight. You have made me see. My friends toward the heavens, I see the holy swirl of the Spotted Eagle Nation.

They have come. They have made me see. My friends toward the Earth, I feel you, the Medicine Nation, gathering around us. They have made me see. Wakan Tanka, Skan Skan (the Most Holy), the Sacred Essence Moving, let my father live this year. The next summer I pledge myself to dance the Sundance for all my relatives."

After the giveaway and feeding of the people, we announced that all was in readiness for the funeral procession to begin. The eight pallbearers assembled along the sides of the casket; they lifted the casket and slowly proceeded to the south door of the house. My niece in her husband's pickup truck was waiting nearby. The casket was gently loaded on the truck bed, and the pallbearers climbed on board and sat on the sides of the truck bed.

I told the truck driver to go slow. Following close behind was another pickup truck carrying a drum and Sundance singers from throughout Lakota country. They were singing traditional Sundance songs. We went south from my mother's home for three-quarters of a mile to the blacktop Highway 18, and from there, we turned right, toward the Black Hills. Within a mile, we approached the Catholic church, with Highway 18 going in between two of its graveyards. We passed the church, went for another mile and a half, and stopped at the turn-off for the road to the Pte Woku Sundance area.

We transferred his body from the pickup truck to the horse-drawn wagon, or buckboard. In spite of the mud, the melting snow, and the growing sadness becoming more and more prominent in all of us in the funeral procession, we still had that sense of kinship which makes the community become strong. Suffering with the pain of our loss, we remained solemn. I glanced around, looking at the people, and in their eyes and through my mind's eye I could feel their encouragement with its loving affinity. Although we were shrouded in grief, we were still one—one people drawn together as this world will one day be.

We had two miles of mud and melting snow yet to go through, with hills and two places to cross where a creek had once been but which now was a dry creek bed full of snow that had been plowed earlier. The team and wagon continued slowly, followed close behind by the truck with the Sundance singers. As I heard the echoing melody of the songs in the valley, I seemed to feel his presence, and knew that he was approving and happy that this day was just as it should be. Our trek was a slow and winding one. Sometimes the team and wagon had to be pushed by hand by the pallbearers and those who chose to walk behind the wagon.

We stopped a hundred yards from the gravesite. From there, the pallbearers and others helped to carry the casket. Those last hundred yards were no easy task. It was then that a thought entered my mind. I remembered a time when my father and I had visited this place, and as we stood on that grassy little knoll, he spoke of times past. He said that when he first married my mother, he had come through here with everything that he owned. This consisted of a team and wagon, plus a saddle horse, and on top of the wagon, there was a plow. Later he used that plow to till a garden for our family and several others. He said that he would rest his body here among the rolling hills and breaks with the large and small pine trees. And there, up above where the dry creek bed is, that is where his last resting place is.

The snow was between ankle and knee deep as we started up the first rise, the former site of a windmill where cattle and horses drank. This flat area below the gravesite is perhaps fourteen yards across. We moved slowly and silently. There were a few people already at the gravesite when we started climbing the steep slope.

The grave was set north to south. Toward the west was a green tobacco pouch flag signifying the Thunder Beings. Toward the north was a red tobacco pouch flag signifying the Buffalo Nation. Toward the east was a yellow tobacco pouch flag signifying the Elk Nation. Toward the south was a white tobacco pouch flag signifying the Gray Swan Nation. All flags were set in the ground seven yards from the grave itself. On the south side, between the flag and the grave, we had erected a scaffold and placed upon it in the shape of a man a bundle into which we had put his personal belongings.

I was standing southeast of the grave between the yellow and white tobacco pouch flags. The casket was brought to a stop between the white and green tobacco pouch flags. It was slowly taken clockwise to the east with its yellow tobacco pouch flags. Then it was brought into the *hocoka* (circle). Within the hocoka at the east was a fire that had been tended for some time, and some rocks had been heated in the fire earlier. The casket was purified by putting water upon the heated stones, while the pallbearers held the casket above the heated rocks and the rising steam. The casket was then taken to the grave, where it was gently lowered to rest upon four iron bars above the grave pit.

The Sundance singers began the Sacred Pipe filling song. The assistant draped a red cloth over the casket. I called to a nephew who had given this holy man a beaded case and knife to take with him. I put it on the casket near the bowl of water that was also there. The assistant began to light the twisted sweetgrass braid and to smudge the simple altar of the Sundance Nation. By doing this we envision the reality of Wohpe, and when we smell its lovely fragrance, our thoughts transcend to Her. The Lakota oyate know and feel Wohpe as a medium—with Her is beauty beyond compare, and compassion of the heart. Her Father, Wakan Tanka, gave to her the powers of a goddess.

As he finished filling the sacred Pipe he motioned to me to receive the sacred Pipe, and I then received it. Next, he motioned to my two sisters to hold a separate white flag, outstretched lengthwise, at the south. This white flag signifies the Spirit Trail and once torn in the middle, the deceased is left to travel the Spirit Trail to the Land of the Winds. My sister Cynthia and her sister tore the cloth, as my brothers Paul and Isaac stood silently upright in agreement, while I held the sacred Pipe, ever upward, ever pointing toward the Spirit Trail.

Then I told a nephew who lives nearby to ignite the scaffold and I motioned to the Sundance singers for them to start singing the traditional Sundance songs of the Sundance Nation. It was then that I sensed him near the grave, dancing to the beat of the drum. My spirit was filled with silent majesty, the ecstasy of joy. I was overwhelmed to know that he was happy, the final true happiness one can hope to attain, the love of the Great Spirit.

Peter V. Catches (Zintkala Oyate).

EPILOGUE

By Peter V. Catches (Zintkala Oyate)

Because all of us are human and raised the way we are, we cannot truly decide for ourselves who we want to be. Therefore, by the nature of our birth, we cannot choose our color or our place in society. We cannot change the fact that each and every one of us is unique and that there is a place for us in this Sundance Nation.

I will not live under the shadow of the Sacred Tree. Instead, I will let my soul sparkle in its light and receive the wisdom from the All Conceiving. For God's own love rustles through the leaves of the sacred Tree of Life in His spiritual realm, incomprehensible to our world of light and shadow.

For some, however, it is easy to accept the concept of our sacred hoop being broken, easy to accept that we are individuals who must "assimilate." I cannot and will not accept a way that is not virtuous; I look on and feel the depression and despair gnawing at me. The only thing that overcomes this spiritual depression is the realization that I am a human being with all the liveliness to live in harmony.

The Great Spirit has put me here to live as a part of His creation, to respect the Mother Earth, the sky, the sun, all creatures, and the great wonder of each direction.

Lakota people and other Native peoples who know of the four virtues of the man and of the woman, and who choose to live virtuously, are not wrong. We choose to live this way religiously. This means that the horror of some matters in our lives is not enough of an excuse for refusing to face them. The problem that we face today in dealing with institutional racism is that it has become an integral part of the very fabric of thought itself, and thus supports and moves our society without people being aware of it.

We are under programs that are supposedly working toward the elimination of institutional racism. But it seems that there are those who really do not want this to happen. Instead of being used to eliminate prejudice, the information collected by these programs is used instead to further feed the horrible spirit of racism. The injustice caused by this hideous idea in our society has affected everyone, and I truly believe that it is causing the spiritual depression afflicting millions today. It has prevented us from grasping the true nature of human beings.

As a Lakota living on the Pine Ridge Indian Reservation in South Dakota, I do feel depressed when observing the form of our society. Although I am condemned to live in poverty, yet I hold close in my heart the determination of the original common man, to remain as I am, affirming the traditional and rejecting the modern on ethical grounds. We as a people know of the presence and love of the Great Spirit, and the vital importance of the people coming together and of following the virtues and living in the traditional manner. Choosing to live virtuously is good for the Lakota, and, as my father said many times, we must live that way in our home, in our community, and in the Nation. As it was in the past, so it is now in the present and will continue to be in the future: a Lakota needs to be reminded and reassured of this to possess common self-respect.

Now let me wander back to when I was a boy. When I was young, I was seeking a spirituality that perhaps comes from the dawn of time. Although there are many forms of it, we have to choose for ourselves which path to follow. There are many churches, religions, and denominations, all crying the word of God. This makes the logical mind hesitate. First, you must realize that God is the Great Mystery that cannot be classified nor understood by man. Second, you must realize that people are suffering from a disease that is self-inflicted, and that this affliction is a degeneration of the spirit likely caused by doctrines of man. I know that as a child growing up on the reservation, I had an inferiority complex which led me to believe that I had no right to pray, and that my father (whom I loved so much) was a medicine man the other children at school called a witch doctor and a disciple of the devil, even though my father healed people who were turned away from the hospital because they were considered hopeless.

I remember beautiful days with laughter, caring, and harmony inside the family as I grew. That changed with the beginning of my education. I came to think of myself first and others last. I learned to be crafty and to disguise my feelings for my own benefit. I did not know that these were the first symptoms of the degeneration of the spirit. I would go to church with no feeling, just going through the motions so to speak. Yet, when I went to a Pipe ceremony, I was completely different. I became ebullient and was content from its beginning to its conclusion.

The realization that I belonged in this experiential religion of the Lakota came as a shock to me. Although I denied it at first, because of the years of brainwashing, I knew that within me was an empathy of the spirit that belonged. I then began to help my father at the Sundance. I must warn you that not everyone can do this. For it is a gift from the Great Spirit that a man is chosen and is able to run this Festival of Light, where human beings and all creation become one. The Sundance under the direction of the mediator is propelled to the very nest of creation itself. It is a time when one's spirit is openly seen, heard, felt, smelled, and touched by an equality of all of the living. Although outsiders misunderstand the Sundance, its essence is the hoop of the world, where all the world becomes one community.

At Oceti Wakan we will confront issues of spiritual degeneration in ourselves and mend those inconsistencies in our path toward wholeness. We will look from windows of the present and reawaken that deep traditional voice. We will hear its expressions, feel its impressions in the vastness of our souls, and become complete again.

Living in a world full of prejudice, we have to look inward to find the true nature of ourselves. Now is the time to change and move toward enlightenment, to extinguish our old fears of one another. When this beacon of loving light burns bright in our once dark and lonely domain, we will beat the drums of unity and shout its songs. For here in America, this young nation of diversity, we are destined to attain the complete love of the Great Mystery. I thank you and may the Great Wakan Tanka bless the steps of your path.

Hanbleceya (Pipefast).

NOTES

1. This statement is an indirect reference to two different realities. First, because of the repression imposed on the practice of Lakota spirituality for many years, rites and ceremonies were conducted "behind covered windows" and in "darkness." Such activities went underground in order to prevent action against the Lakota involved by Bureau of Indian Affairs (BIA) representatives (as well as others who would report to the BIA). Second, medicine men of other clans use black medicine (which is also an element of life) in healing and other rites. Spotted Eagle Way medicine men do not.

2. The "deity of the brave" refers to the sacred dream or dreams of a great Lakota warrior of the past, whose spirit lives on in the memory and recollections of the Lakota people. This term is also representative of warriors (past, present, and future) who embody the Lakota Nation's principal virtues of generosity, fortitude, fidelity, and bravery.

3. "Natural conduct" in the Lakota lexicon has the connotation of carrying oneself with dignity. It includes respect of self and other people's boundaries, as well as

respect for all life, or carrying oneself properly on Mother Earth.

4. Individuals vary tremendously in terms of spiritual knowledge and attainment. A spiritual man of the Eagle's Way is capable of knowing people's individual spiritual needs, and helping them accordingly.

5. The Lakota spiritual system is based on understanding of a relationship hierarchy. At the very top is unity, wherein all life is one—pain, joy, and the entire range of needs experienced by an individual is felt by everyone. When unity (peace, harmony) is destroyed or damaged, relationships are guided by compassion, the attempt to empathize with others. When compassion no longer guides relationships, justice without feeling or emotion prevails; that is, a legalistic abstraction of fairness, wherein an individual's uniqueness is ignored. Finally, when even justice without feeling no longer guides relationships, they are reduced to a complete "loss of self." When greed and materialism determine the extent and nature of relationship, everyone and everything in the world are reduced to the status of life-less objects.

6. In traditional matriarchal Lakota society, grandmothers taught grandchildren the fundamentals of life, that is, the ways of the natural world, and proper relationships among people and between people and other forms of life. In the absence of a grandmother, other older members of a child's extended family or clan would assume this responsibility.

7. The 1868 Treaty was broken by the discovery of gold in the Black Hills by an expedition led by General

George A. Custer, after which the U.S. government annexed the land. Beginning in the 1920s, the Great Sioux Nation initiated litigation to have the government comply with the treaty. In 1980, the U.S. Supreme Court ruled that the broken treaty was "a rank case of injustice," and awarded the Great Sioux Nation $119 million (described as market value of the land at the time of annexation, plus interest payments since that date). The money award was rejected by the Nation and at the time of this writing, the case was still in the courts.

8. The book referred to here is *The Sun Dance People: The Plains Indians, Their Past and Present* (New York: Knopf, 1972), written and photographed by Richard Erdoes.

9. See note 2.

10. Much has been written and reported on the Wounded Knee massacre. Most accounts agree that Chief Big Foot was suffering from pneumonia, and most of the people in the camp were physically weak and afflicted with mental and spiritual depression. The Minneconjou band had been disarmed and had agreed to cease all hostilities before camping near Wounded Knee Creek. The band was flying a white flag when soldiers caught up with them on December 28, 1890.

　　Soldiers surrounded the camp on all sides, and set up several large Hotchkiss guns on a hill overlooking the camp. The next day the soldiers systematically machine-gunned nearly every Lakota man, woman, and child in the camp. The soldiers also pursued fleeing women and children, and killed some of them as far as two miles from the site.

Soldiers killed at Wounded Knee were shot by fellow soldiers in the general mayhem of flying munitions. Twenty-seven soldiers participating in the massacre received the Congressional Medal of Honor for bravery. Recently, the efforts of Native Americans to end this travesty of bravery in battle resulted in a decision by the U.S. Congress to "rescind" the medals given to soldiers involved in the 1890 massacre.

11.   Among the grievances publicized by participants in the Wounded Knee seizure were the U.S. government's reneging on numerous rights of the Lakota (and other Native American peoples) articulated in treaties, including the annexation of the sacred Ka Sapa (Black Hills). Statements by AIM at the time specified that the Sioux, like other Native tribes throughout the United States, had ceded land to the U.S. government, and that in payment, the U.S. government had agreed to provide certain goods and services to the tribes. Instead of providing such goods and services, asserted AIM, the federal government had imposed tyranny in a direct fashion via the Bureau of Indian Affairs and other government agencies, as well as indirectly via Native people on the reservations who had adopted non-Native culture, attitudes, tactics, and even violence against traditional members of their own communities.

12.   The words "wopila" and "pilamaya" both mean "thank you." Wopila is also the name of a thanksgiving ceremony, but is not one of the Lakotas' Seven Sacred Rites.

13.   A genuine medicine man attends a pow-wow or other gathering only when invited by the organizers to "say the

main prayer." The medicine man may then remain on site until the end of a pow-wow to retrieve eagle feathers that may fall to the ground, thereby preventing harm to the participants.

14. For the Lakota, the Sundance is an annual rite of renewal, somewhat comparable to New Year's Day in Western culture. The Spotted Eagle Way Sundance takes place on the Pine Ridge Reservation in July.

Petaga Yuha Mani holding the sacred Pipe and eagle fan and praying
to the Great Mystery in Medicine Bow Mountains.

GLOSSARY

agito—enlightenment

akisa—war whoop, or bringing blessing on those who use their voices in the akisa

Anpetu ki le wakan yelo—This is a holy day. Tokahe ya taku wa yelo—I am the first relative of this day. Wanble gleska wan le ya kinyan u welo—A spotted eagle is saying this as he comes. Anukan san wan le ya kinyan u welo—A bald eagle is saying this as he comes flying.

blaheceya—the beginning of healing

Brulé—band of the Tetons

Canku Lute—the Red Road of Life

Cannunpa—Sacred Pipe

Cannunpa Tawooglake—refers to the Pipe Way, in that whosoever respects, loves, honors, and takes care of the Pipe will have a long life

cansasa—Indian tobacco, or red willow bark (side facing trunk) plus medicine

catkuta ukea—from the back it comes

ehake eyokpaza—the last dark portion of the night before the first light of dawn

eyokipisni—unhappy

Hanbleceya—Pipefast

heyoka—a person who literally does things backwards in a humorous manner but whose spirit helpers are the powerful Thunder Beings

hocoka—circle

hokahey—a command or message to move

Hunkapi—Making of a Relative

Hunkpapa—Sitting Bull's band of Tetons

Igmu Ska Wan He—When the White Cat Came to Our Camp

Inipi—Purification Rite

initi—purification structure

kakala—grandfather

Ka Sapa—Black Hills

kinnikinnick—See *cansasa*

kinyan u welo—flying as he comes

Lakota—the first people of peace

Le miyaca nawajin yelo—This is I who is standing. Wa mung yanka yelo—Look at me.

lena ota makuye—I want more like this

le yatkan yo a nicisni ktalo—drink this water and you will get well

maka mani ukea—close and on the ground it comes

mitakuye oyasin—all my relations

naca—leader

nagi—spirit

nunpa—two

Oceti Wakan—Sacred Fireplace

Oglala—band of the Tetons, translated as "scattered"

Okawinga Win—Perpetual Cycle Woman

Ota Iyanka—Runs a Lot

Owanka Nasto—song during which everyone present dances around the Sundance Tree that has just been planted

oyate—people

papa—dried meat

Pahan San Oyate—Gray Swan Nation

peji—marijuana

pilamaya—thank you

pow-wow—originally known as Osmaha Wacipa, but is now contest based

Pte Woku—Feeding of the Buffalo

Sihanskala—Long Feet

Skan Skan—the Most Holy

Spaniciya—Burnt Himself

tahansi—cousin

Taku Skan Skan—Most Holy Judge, Sacred Essence Moving

taniga—tripe (buffalo cow)

Tatanka Oyate—Buffalo Nation

Tate Makoca—Land of the Winds

tiyospaye—community

teepee—home

Tetons—Hunkpapa (Camp at the Horn End), Sicunga (Burnt Thigh), Minneconjou (Use Water in Planting), Oglala (Scattered), Sihasapa (Blackfeet), Oohenunpa (Two Kettle), and Itazipco (No Bow)

Tokala society—Kit Fox society, the workforce of Lakota encampments topa—four

Tunkan—In the Purification Rite (Inipi), stones become Grandfathers, or those who have always been and will continue to be. "Tun" translates as "birth," and "kan" as "aged."

Tunkasila—Grandfathers (spirit world)

Tunkasila, Wakan Tanka, onsimilaye ikce wicasa unsiya makakija. Mi takuye kakijapi wakin ya. Ikca wicasa ta cannunpa wan yuha. Hoye ciciye.—Grandfathers, Great Mystery, have pity on me. For, as a common man, I am having a hard time. I carry the burden of my relatives with the common man's sacred Pipe. I implore you.

Tunkasila wa mung yanka yo—Grandfathers, look at me

tunska—nephew

unci—grandmother

Wakan Tanka—Great Mystery, Great Spirit, The Most Holy, God

Wakan Tanka wopila ecece ye ye lo. Wakan Tanka wopila ecece ye ye lo. Wakan Tanka wopila ecece ye lo hey ho. Cannunpa wan yuha wacece la unko amayalupta ca pilamaya ya ya lo. Wakan Tanka wopila ecece ye lo hey. Mitakuye oyasin. Great Mystery, I thank you. Great Mystery, I thank you. Great Mystery, I thank you. With this sacred Pipe, I have asked you and you have answered; I thank you. Great Mystery, I thank you. For all my relations.

wakanyeja—sacred being, child

Wakinyan—Thunder Beings

wakunka—elders

wanble gleska—spotted eagle

wanble gleska weyaka—spotted eagle feathers

wanji—one

wasa—red paint made from clay and fat

wasicu—white men; originally "fat takers"

wasna—dried meat, ground with chokecherries

wateca—portion of food taken home from a feast

wcyaka feathers

Wicasa Wan Kaiglaglag—Radiantly Golden Man

Wiwangyang Wacipi—the Sundance; gazing at the sun they dance

Wohpe—daughter of Taku Skan Skan. Pte San Win (Gray Calf Pipe Woman) from antiquity, who brought the Lakota the Seven Sacred Rites

wojapi—berry pudding

wopila—This word means "thank you," and is also the name of a thanksgiving ceremony (not part of the major Seven Sacred Rites)

yamni—three

yuwipi—tied

zaptan—five